PRAISE FOR
YOU ARE PSYCHIC

"Char is the mentor we all deserve. In *You Are Psychic*, she skillfully and compassionately helps you evolve those little whispers in the back of your mind into full-blown psychic intuition."

—Chris Colfer, award-winning actor and #1 *New York Times* bestselling author of The Land of Stories series

"Char has the biggest heart and a real love for people. She is truly interested in helping others. In her new book she teaches you to understand your intuition and listen to your inner voice to make the wisest decisions to be the best you can be. A must-read!"
—Kathy Hilton

"Shh—do you hear that? It's your inner voice! It's telling you that you are ready to unleash *your* inner intuition, that Char is the perfect guide, and that this is the best book!"

—Ross Mathews, bestselling author
and television personality

YOU
ARE
PSYCHIC

ALSO BY
CHAR MARGOLIS

Questions from Earth, Answers from Heaven

Discover Your Inner Wisdom

Love Karma

*Life: A Spiritual Intuitive's Collection of
Inspirational Thoughts*

The Universe Is Calling You

YOU
ARE
PSYCHIC

7 Steps to Discover
Your Own Psychic Abilities

CHAR
MARGOLIS

ST. MARTIN'S
ESSENTIALS
NEW YORK

First published in the United States by St. Martin's Essentials, an imprint of St. Martin's Publishing Group

YOU ARE PSYCHIC. Copyright © 2022 by Char Communications Inc. All rights reserved. Printed in the United States of America. For information, address St. Martin's Publishing Group, 120 Broadway, New York, NY 10271.

www.stmartins.com

Designed by Devan Norman

The Library of Congress Cataloging-in-Publication Data is available upon request.

ISBN 978-1-250-80504-1 (hardcover)
ISBN 978-1-250-80505-8 (ebook)

Our books may be purchased in bulk for promotional, educational, or business use. Please contact your local bookseller or the Macmillan Corporate and Premium Sales Department at 1-800-221-7945, extension 5442, or by email at MacmillanSpecialMarkets@macmillan.com.

First Edition: 2022

10 9 8 7 6 5 4 3 2 1

This book is dedicated to my angels on Earth
and my angels in heaven. You know who you are!
Thank you for always being there!
I am blessed!

CONTENTS

FOREWORD

My Friend Is a Superhero

Picture it! New York City, 2012!

I was a wide-eyed twenty-one-year-old standing backstage at *Live! With Regis and Kelly!* I anxiously peeked out of the wings like a frightened clownfish as I waited for my cue to walk on stage. The final advertisement in the commercial break played on the video monitors above me—ABC insisted we didn't want to miss the series finale of *Desperate Housewives* that Sunday—and my heart was pounding because as soon as the preview finished, I'd be interviewed live in front of millions of people!

My mind raced as I mentally rehearsed all the talking points about the projects I was there to promote (a children's book, a television show, LGBTQ+ rights, oh my!). The pressure was on and my harsh perfectionism did me zero favors. I convinced myself that if I messed up one word—*just one word*—I'd never get asked on a talk show again.

"Twenty seconds," a stagehand told me. "Break a leg out there."

"Thanks," I said, and nervously gulped.

"By the way, don't be offended if Regis pronounces your

name wrong," the stagehand added. "We consider it a rite of passage."

Suddenly, I was distracted by someone moving out of the corner of my eye. I turned toward the movement and saw another stagehand escorting a pretty blond woman in a cheetah-print coat. The stagehand guided her to a discreet corner backstage and giddily gestured for all the surrounding crew members to be quiet.

"Who's that?" I asked.

"That's Char Margolis. The producers are sneaking her on the show after your segment."

"Why?"

"It's Regis's final year so they're surprising him with memorable guests."

"Her name sounds familiar."

"She's a famous psychic-medium. The last time she was on the show she predicted Kelly's pregnancy before she had told anyone. It was wild."

As if I weren't stressed enough already, my whole body went stiff. *I was terrified of psychics!* Thanks to the books I'd read and movies I'd watched over the years I had unfairly associated all psychics, mediums, mystics, and clairvoyants with *bad news*. I instantly thought of the witches from *Macbeth*, Professor Trelawney from the Harry Potter series, Tangina Barrons from *Poltergeist*, and the damning prophecies they gave their stories' protagonists.

Char sensed my fearful gaze and sent me a friendly wave. I quickly looked in the opposite direction and pretended I didn't notice her. *We couldn't engage!* What would I do if she gave me a grim prediction? What if she told me all the projects I was working on were going to fail? What if all that hard work was for nothing? I decided the best thing to do was avoid her at all costs. After all, no news is good news, right?

"Get ready," the stagehand whispered. "You're on in five . . . four . . . three . . ."

"Our next guest is an award-winning actor and soon-to-be published author. Please welcome Chris Colfer."

Holy smokes. *Regis Philbin got my name right!* The stagehand pulled open the curtain and the studio audience greeted me with a welcoming applause. I took a seat on the stool across from Regis and Kelly Ripa, and the interview began. It went well—at least, I think it went well. The adrenaline rush made it hard to focus, but I managed to promote all my projects and make a few jokes without spontaneously combusting or projectile vomiting—a victory in my book.

The interview finished, the audience politely applauded, and the show went to another commercial break. I thanked Regis and Kelly profusely for having me, I waved goodbye to the crowd, and the stagehand escorted me backstage. I was so overwhelmed from the interview I completely forgot Char was hiding backstage until I walked directly past her. We made close eye contact and I gasped.

"Great interview, honey," she said. "You are so adorable."

"Th-th-thanks," I stuttered.

"Where do you live?"

"La-La-Los Angeles."

Char placed a comforting hand on my shoulder and gave me a kind smile.

"Before you leave, I just want to tell you what a huge fan I am of yours and everything you're doing. Especially for my friends in the gay community. You're in this world to help people. And I'm here for you if you ever need anything."

"I . . . I . . . I appreciate that."

"I'd love to give you a reading when you're back in Los Angeles. I live there part-time."

Before I could respond, the stagehands ushered us apart, and like ships in the night, Char and I went our separate ways. Once I was back in my dressing room, I let out a long sigh of relief. I was thrilled the interview had gone smoothly, but even better, I was thankful I had encountered my first psychic without receiving any tragic news. However, Char had been so sweet and warm, I couldn't help wondering if my perception of her—and of all psychics in general—was misguided. Perhaps mediums weren't so scary after all?

Picture it! Beverly Hills, 2013!

More than a year later, I was backstage at the Saban Theatre shooting an episode of the television show *Glee*. Lea Michele, Naya Rivera, Sarah Jessica Parker, and I were sitting in our cast chairs waiting for a lighting setup. There's always a lot of time to kill on a film set, and that day the girls and I chatted about everything from composting to the Hubble telescope. Eventually, the subject of psychics came up and we discussed our personal experiences with them. If memory serves me correctly, Sarah Jessica had seen a few psychics over the years with varying results. Lea was singing the praises of a psychic she had just seen on *The Real Housewives of Beverly Hills* and was in the process of booking an appointment. I don't believe Naya was interested in the subject and, like me, she admitted to being a little afraid of them.

"You know, I met a famous psychic last year on *Regis and Kelly*," I said. "She was so nice and offered me a reading, but I never took her up on it. I'm really kicking myself now—it would have been a great story."

The day after my co-stars and I talked about psychics—not the next *week* or the next *month* but the very next day—*Char Margolis reached out to me*! I opened my phone to find an email from my publicist with the subject *Psychic Reading???*

"Hey, Chris," my publicist wrote. "Did you meet a psychic named Char Margolis backstage at *Regis and Kelly* last year? Her people reached out to us to let you know her offer for a reading still stands. Would you like us to respond?"

I stared at my phone screen for a good five minutes without moving a muscle. I was shocked! I was bewildered! I was *spooked*! It was such a profound coincidence I knew it was far more than *just* a coincidence. So, naturally, I emailed my publicist back and booked my very first psychic reading with Char.

As expected, I was absolutely terrified during our first session. I sat across from her and tightly clutched a pillow until my hands went numb. Char was incredibly patient with me and gently walked me through her process and what to expect. She closed her eyes, said a prayer of protection around us, and went into her zone. At this point, thanks to the notoriety of *Glee*, a plethora of information about my past and personal life had been made public. Anyone with an internet connection could easily find out where I lived, how many siblings I had, where I went to high school, what projects I had on the horizon, etc. I went into our reading very hopeful but also a little skeptical about what she might tell me. However, what Char channeled that afternoon was nothing short of extraordinary. She tapped into information that no one could have possibly known without a direct line to the other side.

During the reading, Char connected to a woman named Cynthia whom I was very close to when I was a child. She knew Cynthia had died of breast cancer when I was twelve and she knew we used to binge episodes of *Xena: Warrior Princess* together while she recovered from chemotherapy. She let me know that Cynthia was watching over me and was very proud of everything I had accomplished. Char also channeled my late grandfather and she knew he had been a pastor and was quite the family jokester. My grandfather told Char that he was responsible for my sense of humor and even asked her to "pull his finger" so I would know it was really him. Char knew I wasn't happy in my current house and told me I would be moving soon. She described in great detail, down to the square footage and shape of the pool, the house that I ended up buying just two months later.

I was so stunned by everything Char told me I barely spoke a word in our session. To my surprise, the reading hadn't been the laundry list of doom and gloom I'd expected. On the contrary, it was an hour of happy reunions and positive reinforcement. She completely changed my perspective, not only on psychics, but on life and the afterlife in general.

However, the greatest thing to come from our meeting was the fantastic friendship Char and I developed over the following year. I don't know what she saw in the nervous young man sitting across from her that day—she certainly didn't *need* an anxious, high-pitched twenty-one-year-old in her life—but for whatever reason, Char took me under her wing and has been encouraging me, mentoring me, and mothering me ever since.

If someone made a movie about Char's and my friendship it would be a hilarious, supernatural buddy comedy. We've gone searching for extraterrestrials under the starry night sky of Joshua Tree, we've been each other's dates to museum openings and drag shows, we've spent hours gossiping about the royal family while consuming pounds of Chinese food, and on a few occasions, Char has even refereed arguments between me and my deceased relatives. Having a friend like Char is like having a superhero on demand. If I had a nickel for every time she's helped me find my lost keys or remember a forgotten password, I'd be rich. Though the absolute best part about being friends with Char Margolis is having a front-row seat to her incredible work.

Over the last decade, I've seen Char literally save lives by predicting medical issues before they occurred. I've seen her bring comfort and peace to the heartbroken and grief-stricken with messages of love and forgiveness from the beyond. I've been a guest on her podcast, *CharVision*, where she brings a wealth of inspiration and positivity to an international audience. I've seen her passionately inspire and champion others, including myself, to use intuition to prevent problems and achieve goals. And as a testament to her good heart, I've watched her turn down big opportunities that promised fame and fortune for smaller projects that respected her and her priorities.

"Char, why did you say no? That's a *huge* show!"

"Because it's not about me, it's about helping people and getting the work out there," she's told me many times.

So, for anyone who has picked up this book hoping to develop or understand their own psychic abilities, you've come to the right place. There is no one in the world who is more passionate or devoted to helping people through the benefits of intuition than Char Margolis. Within these pages, she will effortlessly and selflessly teach you how to use your intuition as a compass to navigate the challenges of day-to-day life. And if you're as lucky as me, by the time you finish this book, Char will have given you an entirely new perspective on the universe and the messages it's sending you.

To put it simply, Char is living proof that there is more to life than life. Enjoy!

—*Chris Colfer*

AUTHOR'S NOTE

Dear Reader,

As I write this, I have been sequestered at my home in Palm Springs for more than two weeks because of COVID, and I am finally sitting down to start my next book, *You Are Psychic*. Earlier today, I went for a walk and called my sister Elaine on Face-Time so she could enjoy the mountain views, manicured lawn, and fruit trees. It's a comforting feeling during lockdown to know there is an abundance of citrus trees outside my window. The virus has given a whole new meaning to appreciation and the value of life as we know it.

I noticed some butterflies and kept trying to capture them to show my sister. Our mother's spirit comes to us as a butterfly. She kept saying, "I see another one," as I tried to capture them on my iPhone. What a surprise I just had looking out my window! Hundreds of butterflies have been passing my window for the last twenty minutes! They must be migrating—an amazing sign for me that our loving mother is still with us, watching over us, and happy that I'm starting my new book! I procrastinated for two weeks. I finally felt motivated to get started and *BAM*—the sign of the butterflies manifested before my eyes.

The last time this happened to me was about four months after my mother crossed over to the spirit world. I was hiking at Fryman Canyon in LA. It was early in 1999, so not everybody had smartphones yet (at least, I didn't), and I asked my

XX   **AUTHOR'S NOTE**

mother for a sign. As I walked up the hill that I had hiked hundreds of times before, I saw thousands of butterflies. I stretched out my arms and could feel their fragile wings fluttering on my arm. *Yikes! It's a bug!* I thought and put my arms down, but quickly raised them and thought, *But it's my mom!* There was one other girl on the mountain, and I said, "Do you believe this?" She was equally amazed. I wanted to make sure it wasn't my imagination.

Many spirits take the form of nature to connect with us. It was Elaine who first noticed the sign for our mother was a butterfly. Elaine was in her garden thinking about Mom, and a butterfly kept landing on her. She called me up and told me that she thought Mom came as a butterfly! That's how we figured out what her sign is for us! Elaine was the one who was psychic and aware.

You can imagine how elated I am at this moment watching the migration of these beauties! I get signs from my loved ones in spirit all the time. My family and close friends do as well!

I am writing this book to help you understand that you can experience these moments of psychic connection. You can experience when your loved ones are trying to reach out to you from heaven. You have psychic abilities that you might not even be aware of, even if you have had glimmers and glimpses of them in the past. As I write, I am blessed to have such an incredible experience, especially during this time of crisis in our world. I'm hoping you will learn to use the material in this book to prevent problems, attain goals in your life, and appreciate the beauty of life in and around you.

We live in a physical world, and we live in an energetic world. You can learn to understand this "sixth sense" and find out what signs the Universe, as well as your loved ones in spirit, are telling you. They want you to know right now, as you are reading this, that they are loving, protecting, and watching over you.

This book will show you how to connect like never before, so that you know that you are psychic and that you are not alone.

Love,

Char

YOU
ARE
PSYCHIC

INTRODUCTION

How I Discovered I Was Psychic

I knew things before they happened when I was a child. When I was four years old, my father took me grocery shopping. When we returned home, my mother looked over the bill as she always did, being the bookkeeper in the family. "That lady cheated us," I said. My mother looked over the bill and discovered that indeed the shopkeeper had overcharged us. To be clear, at that age, I could barely count to ten—I certainly didn't know how to add or review receipts, but I did have an overwhelming feeling of being cheated. From that day on, we called the small market "the Cheaters."

Two weeks later, my mother took me out for lunch. I loved burgers and fries (I still do). The waitress brought us the bill. I said, "Mommy, that lady cheated us." The great thing about my parents is that they didn't dismiss me—or, more important, dismiss my feelings. I bring this up because children have a purity of gut. What I mean by this is that while children may make up stories or tease their siblings or at times misbehave, most children have not yet learned to discount what they feel. If a child is telling you they have a bad feeling about someone, I strongly encourage you to listen. They may not have the words to articulate why, but that purity of gut, which later in life we so frequently discount as irrational, can be what saves us.

There are more important feelings than a love of french fries (although my taste buds might disagree), but after I voiced my concern to my mother, she looked at the bill, and the woman had overcharged us by ten cents. It may seem insignificant now—sixty-six years ago, ten cents was about the price of a cup of coffee—but the significance of my mother validating first my feelings and then the accuracy of them was a pivotal step in me learning to trust those feelings.

When I was eight years old, someone broke into our house. A couple of weeks later, I woke up in the middle of the night and saw an apparition of a man in rags. I could actually see through him. He had a pouch in one hand. He took his other hand and dipped it into the pouch.

I was scared to death. I pulled the blankets over my head. I peeked over the covers. Before my eyes, I saw him sprinkling glittering, golden lights on me. As they landed, they evaporated. I threw the blankets over my head again and started pinching my arm to see if I was sleeping. The next morning, I ran into the kitchen, where my mother was making breakfast.

"Mommy, Mommy, the burglars were here again last night." I told her the story about the man in rags that I could see through and how the brightest golden lights showered my body. My mother was so wise! She said, "Oh, honey, that was just the Sandman!"

"The Sandman?" I replied. "I didn't know there was a Sandman!" He helped people sleep! There even was a song about him called "Mr. Sandman." So it made perfect sense to me.

My sister Dr. Alicia Tisdale is very psychic and absolutely brilliant. She has a Ph.D. in psychology, and also counsels people through past life regressions. We were recently talking about that experience with the lights, and she said that might have been when the angels solidified my gift. The great thing about my family, my parents and two older sisters, is that they completely supported my feelings, my visions, and my insights.

However, from that night on, I was afraid to sleep alone. I kept feeling energies around me that I could not see. Someone had to stand in the doorway of my room, and I had to keep a light on. My sisters are nine and thirteen years older than I am. They married young and were out of the house by the time I was eleven. I even went to summer camp every year so I wouldn't be alone. It was a horseback riding camp. I eventually ended up running the camp as the head counselor!

I went to college and lived at home with my parents. I started at a junior college. One of the courses I took was snow skiing. Yes, you heard me right, snow skiing—finally, a class I loved! It was there that I met my husband. I was standing in line for the chairlift. Riding the chair with other people helps the line go faster in the freezing-cold weather.

"Is anybody single?" I said. A tall, dark-haired man said, "I am." Two years later, neither of us were—single, that is. It was a whirlwind romance. He flew me to New York City for the day, took me to Tiffany's, and said, "Will you marry me?" He asked me to pick out a ring straight out of *Breakfast at Tiffany's*, where he got the idea. He was ten years older than I was, and I was smitten! He took me to Central Park, where he bought me a rose and took me on a buggy ride around the park. When we were done, we put the rose in the horse's bridle. We went to Mama Leone's for lunch and then to see a matinée of *Man of La Mancha* with the original cast (including Richard Kiley)!

We took the last plane back to Michigan, and I was home at my parents' house in my own bed that night. We had a beautiful wedding. My parents went all out! My friends and family

were all there. Even one of my teachers was there. The sanc-
tuary was magnificent—a huge round room held up by pillars,
with a gorgeous star in the ceiling.

The reason I'm telling you this story is important. As the
doors opened to the auditorium, I saw my adoring father waiting to walk me down the aisle and the man I loved waiting for
me to be his wife. As the organ started playing the wedding
march, I had the overwhelming feeling that this marriage was
not going to work. I didn't know how I could have this terrible
thought at this incredible moment in my life, so to help push
the thought away, I started to skip down the aisle.

Now, in those days, marriages were very serious ceremo-
nies. It was simply not done that a bride would dance or even
think of skipping down the aisle. As I look back at that experience, I know this was a psychic feeling.

One of the reasons I am sharing this with you is that I am
not unique in having this feeling on my wedding day. I don't regret getting married; as someone who makes a living as a medium, I tend not to look back at the past with regret. There were
lessons I needed to learn, and I am grateful for all of them. I
call this experience out because so many people tell me of their
experiences when their guts gave them clear signals. "I had a
feeling when I walked down the aisle . . ." "I had a feeling before I got in the car . . ." "I had a feeling something wasn't right
with my breast . . ."

One of the lessons from all of this? Listen to your gut!
Sometimes it is at big moments, like a wedding day, but other
times, there are small thoughts that might feel intrusive or silly.
Sometimes they are. I'm psychic, and I probably have more
thoughts I should dismiss than most people have (french fries,
anyone?), but I'm experienced enough to distinguish the
thoughts that are distracting versus those feelings that come

from my gut. I certainly would have appreciated my guides tipping me off a little sooner than when I was walking down the aisle, and it's possible, when I think back, that they did, but I was not yet in a position to hear them or listen to them. I did not understand my intuition yet. This book will help you gain that experience.

Back to my story . . . and more lessons . . .

The first year of our marriage was good, but as time moved on, we grew apart. I met people who were involved in spiritualism. They had séances every weekend, and soon, I began going to them. We gathered in a pitch-black basement with window coverings held up with duct tape. There could not be any light peeking through. It was in a bit of a dangerous neighborhood in Detroit, Michigan, in the '70s. I was scared to death, but not because of the neighborhood. I was scared because we were sitting in the dark, waiting for an apparition!

We sat in this pitch-black room for hours on end waiting to see spirits. Imagine me, afraid of the dark, grasping for dear life, holding on to my seat until my fingers hurt. What better way to conquer my fear of feeling energies and spirits than to face them straight on!

We got to know each other during these séances, and people kept saying I had a psychic gift. At one point, I was asked to read for a stranger. To my surprise, I "knew" things I couldn't have known about her. For instance, I knew she was having problems with her husband and told her his name. I saw spirits standing with her, and I knew their names. I had never met this woman before that evening. She validated everything during the reading to be true.

I always knew I was supposed to do something important with my life but wasn't sure what it was. At that moment, I had an epiphany that changed the course of my life forever. My life's work was to be a psychic, reading for people, connecting with the spirit world, and finding ways to help others heal and move forward with spiritual guidance. I have dedicated my life to this pursuit ever since.

While I was ecstatic that I had figured out my path in life, my husband was not as thrilled. I don't know if he was intimidated by my gift or by my growing confidence, or if he just didn't understand. Whatever the cause, he said, "The day you take money for readings, I'm getting out the divorce papers."

I didn't know what to do. I loved my husband, or I thought I did, but I also knew I had a calling. Again, I encourage anybody who is in a relationship—whether it is intimate (a friend or family member) or with a business or other creative endeavor—who feels obligated to stay despite what their gut is telling them, to please not dismiss their gut. Someone who truly supports you should at the very least respect your gut feelings. You don't have to agree, but you do need to acknowledge that a gut feeling may be even deeper than you realize; it may be your spiritual guides asking you to be open and follow the signs that they are laying out for you—you just need to learn to be open enough to see them. As I couldn't and didn't want to stop my readings or my spiritual growth, my husband and I divorced.

During those days in the séances, I learned a lot. We sat in a dark room for hours every Friday and Saturday night, waiting for spirits to appear. The leader was a trance medium. She would go into a trance, and other entities would speak through her. (I advise that you don't practice this at home, for reasons that will be apparent later on in this book.) Some were wise guiding energies, but some of the energies were not as good. I didn't know that at the time, as I was obsessed with learning all that I could about this other world and my eagerness came with a certain amount of naivete. I am still as eager to learn as I was then, but I have learned to recognize different types of energies. The energies that came through our leader each had their own personality, and her voice would literally change as different entities spoke through her.

The main spirit was her spirit guide named Red Feather. Red Feather seemed to lead the sessions. Sometimes we would sit in this room, explaining what we were psychically feeling and seeing for hours, before he decided to make his appearance. He definitely had an ego. Many years later, I wrote in my book *Questions from Earth, Answers from Heaven* that ego stands for "edging God out"! That should have been my first clue, but I was enamored with this new spirit world that I was discovering and didn't want to impose any judgment on what I was experiencing.

This was one of my early mistakes. Listening to your gut and following your spirit guides does not mean you should abandon your critical thinking skills. Quite the opposite— listening to your gut is the first step, but then applying reason to your gut is where the true learning happens. When you use logic and common sense with your intuition, you get your best answers. I actually took my mother and sister Alicia to a couple of the séances. They saw that I was blossoming as a psychic and growing with my abilities, so they gave it the benefit of the doubt. Red Feather called Alicia the little lady with the big brain. (She's only four foot ten.) My father wanted nothing to do with it. He was always insightful. I think somehow he knew that something wasn't pure.

The teacher started to express that were it not for her, I wouldn't have this gift, and I was naive enough to believe her. *My goodness,* I thought, *if this person brought out my abilities, imagine how others could get help and develop their abilities!* I started bringing her students. She had been a director and fund-raiser for a children's charity. She decided to have me become the publicity person and actually had me volunteering, opening doors at radio and TV stations in Detroit, to publicize the charity events she hosted.

We hosted a billiard bash with the legendary Minnesota Fats. I would take him around to radio and television stations. I had the hardest time chaperoning him. He kept trying to hit on me in the elevators. One day at the WWJ radio station in Detroit, Steve Still, one of the hosts, asked what I did.

I said, "I'm a secondary school teacher, but I'm learning to be a psychic."

He asked, "Would you come on my show and talk about that?"

I said, "Yes, I would be happy to!"

He asked if he could come to my home with a tape recorder. I answered yes, but my gut was telling me that I was supposed to go down to the radio station, because there was someone else there I needed to meet.

At the time, I still didn't trust my gut or my voice enough to speak up, so we went with the plan as intended, and he came to my home. It was a great interview, I read for him, and he seemed genuinely interested in what I had to say. The next day, he called to tell me that the tape recorder was blank! He said it had worked perfectly the day before and worked well after he left, but when he went to review our conversation, nothing had been recorded.

Now I knew for certain what was intended—my guides were making sure that I went down to the station this time. When I arrived at the station to redo our interview, I was committed to being open to whatever happened. After our interview, Steve introduced me to another radio host named John

Delle-Monache. Steve told him how impressed he was with my reading, and John asked if I would be a guest on his show. I said yes and then headed out to a ski-a-thon for para-skiers. I had learned to ski on outriggers, which are like Canadian crutches with ski tips on them. I taught children without a leg to ski. It was one of the most rewarding experiences I have had in my life. After that, my passion for skiing and how restorative it could be for the body and the mind continued to grow. As part of my publicity job, I had the opportunity to suggest guests for the ski-a-thon we put on. I booked famous skiers and helped get them on radio and TV in Detroit to promote our event.

The producers remembered me and kept asking me to go on the air and do my psychic work. (This was a time when there were only four networks.) I appeared on the local Detroit CBS station with veteran anchorman Vic Caputo. It was my very first appearance on television. He was kind and support-ive. After my experience with Vic Caputo, I appeared on *Kelly and Company*, which was the most popular morning show in Detroit and competed with the national morning shows. John Kelly and Marilyn Turner were wonderful hosts. I was able to read for people in the audience and take phone calls.

By this time, my phone was ringing off the hook. I was on a mission to help people alleviate their fears. Two of the biggest fears people have are fear of death and, ironically, fear of life. I can help people become less fearful of death because I know that we see our loved ones again when we cross over to the spirit world. Fear of life is more complex, but a lot of it has to do with the worries that you, or someone you love or care about, are making the wrong choice or choices. I can help people become less fearful and more confident in their path because I know that we all have the gift of intuition. This gift, our intuition, or our gut, can help us prevent problems and attain goals in our lives. This passion, to help people learn to live with less fear, has always been my mission, and I will do my best to honor it in my lifetime and beyond—in my afterlife.

One day after appearing on *Kelly and Company*, I asked the producer if there was a local talk show in LA. He said it was called *A.M. LA*, hosted by Regis Philbin. If I was supposed to share this work on a bigger scale, and if I did well on TV in LA, then I would know my purpose was to share my work around the world. I went home and called information in LA. You have to realize that we only had landlines then. Every long-distance call was expensive. I asked the operator if I could have the number of *A.M. LA*.

She said, "Honey, what I think you want is KABC."

"Okay, then, I'll take that number," I said. So I called KABC and asked the operator who the executive producer of *A.M. LA* was. She said it was Mr. Ron Ziskin. I thanked her, hung up, and immediately called back and asked for Mr. Ron Ziskin.

Ron would later say he had no idea why he took my call. Executive producers don't take cold calls from anybody—but somebody was looking out for me. They had me do a reading for his associate producer, Donna Lusitana. After I read for her, she asked if I could wait a minute on hold. I could feel the dollars adding up as the minutes ticked by. I knew the reading had gone well, but I didn't know that while I was on hold, she was sharing her experience with Ron and campaigning for me to appear on the show.

Donna came back to the phone and asked if I could get out to Los Angeles. I had never been there before. "Yes!" I said quickly, before she could change her mind or I could think things through. After we hung up, I went to my cowboy boot. Why my cowboy boot, you might ask? Well, that was where I hid my savings. I took out the cash and discovered I had just enough to fly to the West Coast.

When I arrived, a limousine was waiting, and they put me up at the Beverly Wilshire Hotel! I felt like a movie star. In my regular life, I lived on a farmhouse in Michigan in the middle of ten acres. Hollywood was a whole new world for me! All the celebrities would wake up in the morning and watch *A.M. LA.* Everyone said to me, "If Regis likes you, you will make it in this business." They meant the TV business. It was a daunting thing to hear, because at the same time, I interpreted this to mean, "If he doesn't, then you won't."

I was blessed that Regis liked my work! Cyndy Garvey, his cohost, was equally kind to me. Their phones rang off the hook with people trying to track me down. The poor operator! They were inundated with calls. I became a regular guest on the show, and they flew me out to LA every month. I finally had to get an apartment so I could see clients when I came out. Now, Michigan will always be my home, and I love my house there, but that little studio apartment I got thirty-eight years ago is still the home I work out of when I come to LA!

I became a regular on *A.M. LA.* I remember getting ready to do my segment, and a tall man with a familiar face came up to me and said, "Hi! I'm Ed McMahon." I was so excited! Everyone knew that he was the sidekick for Johnny Carson. "I really like your work! Very impressive," he added. I almost fell over. Doc Severinsen, the music conductor for the show, acknowledged my work as well and gave me permission to say he was one of my clients.

One day, I decided I should be on *The Merv Griffin Show.* I was so young; looking back, I can't believe how much moxie I had. I found a connection to the show, and through them,

I met Merv, who was a charming man. He was responsive and respectful of my work and believed in my abilities. I read for him, and his producers booked me. I was never so frightened in my whole life! Merv's show was a very big deal back in those days, and my parents flew to Los Angeles from Michigan. I remember seeing my mom and dad in the audience, grinning ear to ear. I started hyperventilating. I almost fainted. Somehow I read for a couple of people in the audience without blacking out. I will never forget that experience as long as I live!

The most gratifying part of all of this was that I started meeting people and reading for them in person. I was respected for my work and was helping as many people as I could. I also had built a clientele in Michigan. I would read for them by phone. They would call me, because the long-distance calling at that time was really expensive! I was sharing my work nationally. As I said earlier, all I ever wanted was to help people take away their fears: fear of death, by knowing we see our loved ones again when we cross over, and fear of living, by knowing we all have the gift of intuition that helps us attain our goals and prevent problems in our lives. I am blessed to know my purpose and mission on Earth.

Although I was getting accolades and starting to enjoy a bit of fame and recognition, I knew that it always needed to be about the work. As soon as my young ego got in the way, my guardian angels and spirit guides would get me back in line. I was in New York on a show called *Attitudes*. The hosts were Rolonda Watts and Dorothy Lucey. To this day, Dorothy is one of my closest friends. She tells the story about how when I met her, I said, "You are not going to be at this job very long." Months later, it came true. At that time, I hired an agent named Mark Itkin from William Morris. He called me up one day and said, "Guess what? I got you a show on Lifetime!"

I should have been excited. But instead, I said, "Mark, I truly appreciate this, but I don't think I'm ready for my own show!" I was so worried that if it didn't do well, I would be a flash in the pan and it would stop me from continuing my work. I supported myself and got all my clients from the local morning shows I was on and word of mouth.

I infiltrated the business by going on every morning show in every local market I could. There were and are so many skeptics out there. I would win over the hosts, who were also newscasters of the local shows, and would be asked back as a guest, taking phone calls live on air for readings or reading for audience members. I am grateful to all those local and national hosts for their support and for allowing me to share my gift with others.

Eventually, I did a national pilot in Los Angeles produced by Ron Ziskin, which was centered around me as a psychic. It aired on a Saturday morning but got lost in the shuffle around all the children's programming. I remember everyone in the audience wanted a reading. I was so grateful that the audience showed up, I read for every member of the audience, despite how tired it made me. I was the last one to leave the set. It was taped outside, and as the sun set, I watched all the crew and trailers pack up and leave.

I was commuting from Michigan to Los Angeles. I built a house on my property for the teacher who had introduced me to the spirit world. I also would find students for her. In the beginning, she was helpful to me.

I had two horses, six cats, and a dog. The animals were my children. I don't have children, so taking care of these fur babies was my privilege. My former teacher agreed to take care of the animals for me, but soon she said it was too much for her.

Eventually, she started acting strangely toward me, becoming more and more controlling as time went on. For instance, she insisted on getting someone to live in my house to take care of the horses. At first, I was happy about this, because it meant my Labrador, whom I adored, would have company when I wasn't there. But although I quickly came to feel that I didn't want or need to have someone else live in my home, I didn't stand up for myself to make that happen. Here I was, working day and night to pay for everything, and when I would come home to Michigan, I felt so uncomfortable in my own home that I would stay at my mother's condo. I loved being with my mother, who was an angel on Earth, but I wasn't listening to my gut about what was happening in my own home. Instead, I let my teacher dictate these big decisions for me.

I'm sharing this with you because I think it's important to learn that even psychics can get it wrong! I loved my teacher and wanted to repay her kindness to me, so I didn't listen to my gut that things were not as they should be.

As time passed, my beloved yellow Labrador crossed over to the other side. I rescued another dog on the streets of Hollywood and named her Angel. Angel, who was less than eleven pounds but full of love, would fly with me from LA to Michigan and stay at my mom's with me.

Mom was getting older and started to have health problems. While I was in LA, I would get a feeling about her and fly home just in time when she needed me the most. I am so blessed that I was able to spend such quality time with her. This is another reason I encourage you to listen to your gut. We have a psychic connection to those we love and care about: use it and listen to it. If you think about someone, give them a call. They may need to hear your voice. If you have a feeling someone needs to see you, get there. You will never regret showing up for the people you care about, but I can tell you a lot of the sadness I hear in people's voices is from regret and fear.

While I was listening to my gut and being responsive to my mother, I was blind to the actions of my former teacher. My teacher was still giving classes. Her spirit guide would speak through her and still sometimes give profound messages. But other energies or entities would start coming through her, not all of them positive.

Sometimes we would sit around a card table, and everyone would put their fingertips lightly on the tabletop. In time, the table would start vibrating, and eventually, it would fly up in the air. The spirits would take over the table and answer yes-or-no questions. It would teeter on three legs. We would ask questions, and the table would vibrate once for yes and twice for no.

Here I was in the middle of the inner city in Detroit, down in a dark basement, finding answers to life's questions. I learned a lot in those years. You can see, as I'm sharing these stories with you, that there aren't always exact technical ways to develop your psychic intuition. Much of it comes from life experience, using the tools we learn and applying them to handle life's situations. The future can change at any moment or any second because of someone else's choice or decision, so it's up to us to listen to our wisest selves, and our gut feelings, to know what step to take next.

As you'll learn later in this book, our choices are how we accrue our karma. All my life's lessons, after decades of learning, have brought me to this place. I'm blessed with many successes in my life, but my greatest lessons have been learning from my mistakes.

You know, it's a funny thing. When I was twelve years old, I started teaching horseback riding to students. The first thing

I would teach is how to fall off a horse. Because what happens when you fall off a horse? You need to get right back on or you may never ride again, as the old saying goes. They say you're not a good rider unless you've fallen off a horse at least seven times. I've fallen many times in my life, but I have always been blessed with the strength to get right back up!

Like I tell my students, when you get an intuitive feeling, you can't be wrong. But it's the *interpretation* of that feeling that allows you to find your answer. The most challenging thing in reading is interpreting the messages accurately and with wisdom. Later on, I will share with you the difference between being psychic at random and being psychic on demand.

The spirits that spoke through the teacher had definite distinct voices and personalities. I suppose some psychiatrists might say she was unbalanced. But most of us didn't think so, except that she was very moody.

She went into trance on occasions, and we had to wait for hours for the entities to make their entrance. In the late '70s, Red Feather would talk about computers and electromagnetic energy. He would go around the room and try to help each person by reading for them, seeing their loved ones in spirit, and teach on a universal level where everyone would learn something from it.

I feel that in the beginning, the instructor's intent for good was genuine. But as time went on, she changed and, in my personal opinion, not for the better. She would show what seemed like signs of jealousy toward me. I always tried to be helpful and understanding, but she would become quite mean. It was almost like a dark entity and energy took her over and controlled her.

I remember once, she held Red Feather's energy within her so closely that he wasn't able to come through her. She went to a healer of sorts, who freed him and let him speak again. She was very attached to his energy.

I kept seeing changes in these meetings and didn't always want to go. When you hear people say, "Be mindful of the company you keep," it's true. The energy of others is just that—energy—and it does affect you. Sometimes it's wonderful, like the energy of a dance floor or a celebration—or helpful, like the energy of a group who comes together to help put out a fire or pray together in a religious service. There is the healing energy of a friend, the loving energy of a partner, and of course there is energy that hurts, corrupts, or drains. It is hard sometimes in the moment to recognize more harmful energies, and so again, I encourage you to listen to your gut and practice self-love.

I really can't remember all that went on in that basement, because most of the time, I would fall asleep. It was a group of people who believed in the spirit world and became friends. I hate to admit it, but it was almost like we were obsessed with the class. But no one forced anyone to attend. I just think we all thought that we would learn the secrets of the Earth! We were learning the mystery between life and death.

At that time, there was a positive energy and much healing work that was going on. Actually, the teacher's mother was an energy healer. She was a lovely lady, though the teacher wasn't always nice to her and acted as if she were a burden. The teacher's mother had a trumpet—not like a musical instrument in a band but a séance spirit trumpet. It was built like a megaphone but much thinner. I remember the spirit guide asking the trumpet to take flight. If I hadn't experienced it myself, I would have never believed it! I watched the trumpet as it flew up in the air. It never hit anyone in the face or hurt anybody. Once, it actually flew around my head and shoulders, and I felt a gentle breeze swirling around me. I know it will be hard for people to believe, but we were experiencing physical earthbound energy from spirits and re-creating the séances that were so popular in the mid-1800s in England.

As I recall these experiences today, fifty years later, I'm certain that I am supposed to write about them. As I've said earlier, at the time I was naive enough to think that there was only positive energy in the spirit world. But the spirt world has qualities that are similar to the world we live in every day. The world runs like a battery. There is always a positive and negative charge. Just as in everyday life there are positive and negative people, in the spirit world there are positive and negative energies. I believe with all of my heart that the teacher at first only had positive healing intentions, or she would not have taught me. She helped people connect with their spirit guides and taught many, like me, to learn to trust their intuition.

But somewhere along the way, other unfamiliar energies infiltrated her and our circle. We always said a prayer of protection before every meeting. To this day, I say a prayer of protection before every reading that I give to my clients. Because of my past experiences, I understand how important it is to be aware of the energies around us.

Our teacher had recently done an exorcism on a man who had a demon in him. The man's name was Jerry. He had two personalities. Mostly he was pleasant, but occasionally there was a different side of him. Out of nowhere another personality, a tortured soul, inhabited him and growled like a rabid dog. The teacher referred to the real Jerry as "One" and this impostor entity as "Two." Two was emotionally dependent on Jerry and had no desire to part ways. Jerry was dating a girl who also attended the séance meetings. She was in love with this man, but every so often, this other energy would come through him and be abusive. After several sessions, Red Feather gently and lovingly walked and guided the demon Jerry Two to the white light. Jerry One let go and allowed Jerry Two to go. It was a beautiful event. Jerry Two went to the white light, and they were both freed. It turned out that when Jerry was born, he was a twin, and the other twin never developed. Jerry had an extra bone in his body that the doctors said was from his twin that never formed. Jerry screamed with sadness to let his twin leave. But he knew it was what he had to do.

It was after this experience that Jim, the dark, tortured entity, appeared through my teacher. There was a lovely man in the group named Chuck. He was a loyal friend for more than ten years. He was an electrician and had a heart of gold. He actually rewired my whole house for me. One weekend night, when Red Feather arrived, he told us that he was going to teach us about evil. The next thing we knew, there was a voice hissing through the teacher. This was an entity named Jim. He was a tortured soul living in some kind of purgatory. The goal was to try to help him elevate his soul and free him over the next few weeks. After a few sessions with Jim coming through, though, Chuck the electrician had had enough. We all felt that Jim was there to bring negative energy and didn't want to heal. Chuck completely cut himself off. At the same time, a religious cult, which took 20 percent of members' salaries, was luring him to join. He was desperate to find love in his life. Cults will take lonely people and find someone of the opposite sex to lure their members in. Chuck had a hard time finding a girlfriend, and when a woman showed up and started giving him attention, we all knew what was happening. We just didn't want him to be manipulated. We actually all drove to Ohio to try to save him, but it was too late. He'd made his pledge to them. Around that time, I had a dream that Chuck was on my roof, waving his arms and trying to warn me about someone. I was in denial, but he was trying to warn me about the negative energy that was infiltrating the teacher and Red Feather.

There was a brilliant and kind man in the group named George. On occasion, George would question Red Feather about information that was given to us. I remember the teacher becoming angry that someone questioned what was said in the class. I lost touch with George for many, many years and recently saw him again. It was wonderful to see him. As I always say, life is a school, and we are here to learn lessons. There was much wisdom and insight shared in the class in the beginning. George and I discussed how, through the years, our teacher changed. She went from being positive, someone who wanted to help people, to someone who embodied a much darker energy. She had morals and was an honest person morphing into someone who increasingly pulled us into darker energies. In a later chapter, I will tell you about her near-death experience. It was not what you would hope dying is like, but it also taught me that we resonate with the energy of who we are as we cross over. Again, love, honesty, compassion, and positive energies take us to that place in the physical world and the energetic world. Unfortunately, the opposite is true if your energy is evil, hateful, and demonic. I've seen this happen to more than one person, and it is chilling.

Eventually, the teacher no longer wanted to speak to me. Every time something went wrong in her life, she blamed me, all the while she was living in the home I built for her. At that time, I didn't realize or accept that there were good *and* evil forces in the spirit world.

In Los Angeles, I had become friends with a nightclub owner named Mark, who introduced me to Malcolm. When I met Malcolm, he was living in someone's office in Santa

Barbara, sleeping on the floor. I always called Malcolm a wizard. He delved into magic and knew so much about it. He was also a talented astrologer and card reader. I started referring people to him. In fact, he got so busy that he was able to get his own apartment in Los Angeles. Malcolm and Mark were great friends and very protective of me. However, they started working with magic. I was opposed to doing anything that wasn't pure and protective. Malcolm made oils. He and Mark taught me how to protect myself from negative energies. To this day, I only do protective oils with candles. The protective oil energies I use are for uncrossing, Holy Spirit, and the fiery wall of protection. The uncrossing sends any negative energies back to where they came from. The Holy Spirit takes us to the highest energy of goodness, love, and God. The protection oil makes sure you are protected from any negative energies that may try to invade your space.

As you will hear me say several times throughout this book and in life, the world runs like a battery. There's always a positive and a negative charge. Unfortunately, Mark and Malcolm liked to live on the edge. If they didn't like someone or something, they would use oils that were meant to invade others' energy. As time went on, I grew apart from both of them. However, I certainly learned a lot about good and evil. Innately, I knew to never wish bad on anyone. I suggest you don't either. When they say, "Karma's a bitch," it's not without reason. You don't have to love everyone you meet—as I've said previously, there are dark forces you should avoid—but it's not on you, and it will not serve you well to wish ill on others.

Unfortunately, both Mark and Malcolm got cancer. They passed away within two years of each other. Mark was only sixty-one years old. Malcolm was seventy-three. Let me be clear here that some of the most wonderful humans I have ever known have died of cancer; you don't get cancer because you are a bad person. Malcolm and Mark were not bad people, but over time, they started to work with oils and magic that brought negative energy around others. I find it more than a coincidence that they crossed over near each other. This story isn't about what killed them; it is about the energy they had around them when they died. It's another example of why it's so important to stay in the light and only connect with the energy of positive protection and love.

There are psychics out there that seem to be talented. The problem is many are not always connected with the divine energy. Some of them think they are, but many times, they are not. If their ego gets involved, you'd better turn around and walk the other way. As I wrote earlier, ego means "edging God out." It can be compared to a Ouija board. It will give very accurate answers, and then it will tell the person to do something that's destructive, like to go build a bomb and blow up their school. The devil was a fallen angel. He learned everything about good and turned it to evil. I will share with you later on how to protect yourself from any tricksters that may try to invade your mind, body, spirit, or soul. It has always been through my life's lessons, learning by my mistakes, listening to the Universe, that I have been able to understand the gift that I have turned into an ability to process my psychic intuition and connecting to spirits.

The lesson of this story about my teacher, Mark, and Malcom is that even psychics are susceptible to bad energy. Listen to your gut. If someone is giving you advice, where does your gut tell you that advice is coming from? Sometimes even people we love who are good people give us bad advice as a result of their own jealousies, insecurities, or fears. Listen to your gut when they are giving you advice, and ask yourself where you think their gut is. Is their gut coming from love, or could they be motivated by some other darker energies?

When we talk about the spirit world, we tend to idolize it and talk about spirits, guides, and angels. Spirits and energy can be good or bad. We tend to think that because something comes from the spirit world, it is good; it's extremely important to recognize that if there can be positive energy, there can also be negative energy. Spirits are smart, and there is a lot of trickster energy out there. It's very easy to fall prey to negative energy; it's seductive. You need to be open, but cautious, or you can make yourself vulnerable to the wrong energies. Over time, you can become increasingly susceptible to forces that may not have your best interests in mind. You hear stories that nobody voluntarily joins a cult, enters an abusive relationship, or is conned out of their life savings. In most cases, this happens through a slow erosion of your gut instinct. Something doesn't feel quite right, but the positive energies or your emotions are so strong you discount it. Have you ever heard the expression "Too good to be true"? There's a reason for it. This doesn't mean you can't have amazing fortune, great love, and a strong and healthy spiritual life. You can have all of those things, but they don't come free. You have to put in the work and learn to listen.

1

YOU ARE ALREADY PSYCHIC

~~~~~~

What you will learn in this chapter: Many people think that being psychic is something that is only available to a few people who were born with the gift. Not true! All people are born with innate psychic abilities, and this chapter will show you some of the basic psychic abilities that we all have and may not even call "psychic." I'll tell you some stories about people (including me) who used these tools for good, and also what happens when we ignore them. I want you to begin feeling comfortable in accepting that you already, naturally, have some gifts and tools. The more you are aware of them, the more you can use them in a positive way.

~~~~~~

Did you ever have an experience where you wanted something—thing and your gut told you not to pursue it . . . but you did anyway and later regretted it?

Perhaps it is a person you are attracted to, but inwardly, there is a little feeling that they may be trouble. But you feel they are attractive, and you begin a relationship with them anyway, only to find out that your inward feeling was right all along. How would it have ended up if you had listened to that little feeling? Perhaps you would have found a more positive relationship.

Or perhaps there is a business opportunity you know is iffy and could potentially be negative, but you pursue it anyway. It seemed almost too good to be true, a quick way to gain success or money. But in the end, it didn't work out and perhaps even left you a little (or a lot) worse off than before? The opportunity indeed was too good to be true.

Can you remember a time when this happened to you? Whenever I ask this question to an audience and ask them to raise their hands if they can relate, most people raise a hand quickly.

Now think of a time when you had that same nagging feeling about a person or an opportunity, and you actually listened to it . . . and it turned out you were right! We see the person's true colors or see how the opportunity was really a scheme or trap. When this happens, we sometimes say we "dodged a bullet."

Again, when I ask people in audiences if they have had this experience, many (if not most) hands go up.

Why is this important? Think of this as one of your first intuitive, psychic experiences. Remember it! Remember how you felt when you received that feeling—whether you followed it or not. This was most likely a warning from your spirit guides and guardian angels from the universal knowledge of goodness, love, and your most protective deity. It could also have been a karmic lesson you needed to learn. How many times do you have to put your finger on a burning stove to know that you will get burned? Our angels and guides will do their best to help us; however, we all have free will. The future can change at any second, at any moment, because of our choice or decision or that of someone else. Once we act upon it, it starts that energy in that direction, putting that path in motion. Life is our school, and we are here to learn lessons. Our guardian angels and spirit guides are here to help us learn them.

Do you have a journal or notebook close by? If so, go get it, and have it handy as you read this book, and I'll give you some powerful prompts and ideas to write in it. Making this book interactive and personal will mean that you will have a powerful experience. Got the notebook? Great! This is a good time to make a list of all the occasions when you had a gut feeling about something and didn't listen. Go ahead, really write these down. I'll wait right here while you do.

Next, make a list of the moments where you had a gut intuitive feeling about something and you did listen! Again, I'll wait right here while you do this.

Good. Keep these lists close by, and add to them as more experiences come to mind. These lists help when doubts pop up about whether or not you have any psychic connection. You do. These lists prove it. This book will help to increase it.

There are true stories about people who were supposed to take an airplane flight and, at the last minute, turned around and didn't go because they had an intuitive warning, later finding out the airplane they were supposed to take had crashed. Did you know it was reported that Jackie Kennedy Onassis had a vision that her son John Kennedy Jr. died in an airplane crash? I read that she never allowed him to take flying lessons. After she passed away, he learned to fly his own airplane. On the evening of July 16, 1999, John F. Kennedy Jr. died when the light aircraft he was flying crashed into the Atlantic Ocean off Martha's Vineyard, off the coast of Massachusetts.

We not only get these nudges, these messages, for ourselves, but we get them for our loved ones as well. If people accepted these intuitive warnings that we get as real truths, imagine the number of people who would have prevented accidents or be alive today. I find that many creative people are intuitive, but intuition is certainly not limited to creative people. Quite the opposite. There are businesspeople, teachers, mechanics, scientists, grocery store workers, nurses, real estate brokers, siblings, parents—whoever you are, you can learn to listen to your gut and become more intuitive.

It's important to know that these messages come *through* us, not *from* us. When we are connected to the universal consciousness of goodness, love, and God, then the thoughts of wisdom flow through us. We are so busy with work, obligations, families, and life's challenges that we don't always make room in our thought process to understand, become aware, or acknowledge the information that is coming through.

Oftentimes, the messages we receive go against our desires, and we dismiss them! Who wants to plan an important business trip or personal trip with all the rewards of anticipating a successful time ahead and, when you finally get to the boarding process, a voice in your head says, "This isn't safe. Don't go. Turn around"?

Everyone feels that gut feeling differently. Some people get a weird feeling in their stomach and get nauseous. Some people have a direct thought that is *not* based in fear; it's more of an all-knowing feeling. Some get a thought that is felt in their gut. We all have the responsibility of learning what our warning signs are. Sometimes a loved one will simultaneously get the same feeling and bring it up to you even though you never discussed it with them.

CHAR TIP: NUDGES

Which of the following do you experience that could be your psychic tuning fork? What other ways do you get that feeling from the Universe that aren't on this list?

Gut feelings

Many people literally feel something in the gut when there is a moment of truth that they cannot deny. Whether it is good news or bad news, it is wisdom trying to guide them in the right direction. Once they act upon it, there is a feeling of peace. It's the Universe helping them out.

Nagging thoughts

Do you ever find yourself repeating the same idea over and over again? Our divine guidance is intangible. The only way the message can get to us is if it is drummed into our heads until we realize, "Oh, wow! This is a message." There are times my friends will say, "You sound like the Dustin Hoffman character in *Rain Man*." The thought or words coming out of your mouth continue until you get the message! You wake up in the middle of the night, and you can't get that thought or guidance out of your head.

Stomach upset or nausea

Sometimes that gut feeling gets so prevalent that it causes you to feel sick to your stomach, especially if it is a dire warning. It may be the only wake-up call that will make you aware of the message.

Dreams

Our minds are so full taking care of obligations during the day, it's almost impossible for our guardian angels and spirit guides to get a word in edgewise. The only time it's possible is during our sleep, through dreams. Many times, the dream is symbolic. We can't take it literally. For example, a tooth falling out can mean a loss of something in your life that just happened or is going to happen, like a relationship. Dreams can be psychological or psychic.

Imagination

What is a message from beyond, and what is a figment of your imagination?

How many of you had an imaginary friend as a child or know someone who did? Is it their imagination, or is there really an energy connecting with them? Our imagination comes from thoughts from the Universe and from our daily experiences. Walt Disney had a huge imagination and turned his ideas into a magnificent creative venture that all of us have enjoyed at one time or another. There is a universal consciousness of knowledge and wisdom that we all connect to. Even though our imaginations may seem unbelievable, there can be grains of truth in them that can help us create and also guide us. Practice makes perfect. Your imagination may give you an idea to write a successful song, book, or screenplay, or guide you to start an amazing career, or find the love of your life. Never ignore the thoughts and images that enter your mind or words that come out of your mouth.

Profound things you say

There are times in our lives that we say things that come out of left field. It can go against all logic or go against your emotions. I learned this the hard way. If something comes out of your mouth and goes against your feelings or what you believe to be true, check it out. Don't let your emotions get in the way of the wisdom guiding you. Don't blame someone else but eliminate the reasons why you would be right or wrong. For example, you may have an intuition that your spouse or significant other is cheating on you. (You need to be aware of your own fears or past experiences and psychological state of mind before accusing someone else of this.) You don't want to start an argument unnecessarily or cause distrust. But you can do investigating on your own. Perhaps you feel someone is stealing money from you. You can follow the money trail and find out.

Déjà vu

You have an experience that feels as if you have had it before. Usually, this means that you are in the right place at the right time. It's a meant-to-be moment and says you are on the right path at that time in your life. I also find when this happens, I get a psychic thought about the situation I need to be aware of.

Reading signs

Have you ever had something you really needed an answer for? It may be about a romance working out or a new job. We are desperate for an answer. When this happens, put the thought out into the Universe, and then just leave it alone. Don't dwell on it. As the saying goes: "A watched pot never boils." Within hours or a day or two, you may be thinking of your question. You are stuck in traffic and the license plate in front of you has your initials and the billboard to your right says LOVE IS IN THE AIR or THIS JOB'S FOR YOU. There's your answer!

Nature also likes to communicate to you with signs. While filming my show in the Netherlands, I went to the grave site of a young girl named Meril. I was communicating with her and her family. Just then, a bird flew in and landed on her gravestone. The type of bird was a merle! Many spirits will identify with nature to let you know they are with you. Some come as a butterfly, bird, or dragonfly. I have a friend who asked the Universe for an answer, and a beautiful rainbow appeared. I know someone who asked for a sign, and a cloud above her took the shape of a heart. Others have been walking on the beach and found a stone or shell in the shape of a heart. Think about what your loved one's sign is when they visit.

My friend's father drops dimes. My spirit guide White Feather drops white feathers, even in a snowstorm. Once I was walking to lunch with Regis Philbin in New York City during a snowstorm talking about the white feathers that have floated in the studio while I was on his show. Just then, one appeared drifting in front of us. Some spirits come as ladybugs, dragonflies, deer, flowers, and many other forms of nature.

Smells

A spirit may identify with a scent. It could be your grandmother's perfume, your father's pipe smoke, or your mother's favorite recipe. When you sense this, it means they are around you. They may be trying to give you a message. So be aware of your surroundings and thoughts when this happens to you.

Electrical signs

You may be getting a message through electricity. Spirits like to learn to use this to make themselves known. The light in your room starts flickering. The TV turns on and off by itself, and when it turns on, it's the program you watched with your grandmother before she passed away. Some people have gotten phone calls and texts from their deceased loved ones after they passed.

~~~~~~

If we are not heeding the call, our angels and guides will find someone else to make us aware. I do believe that some things in life are predestined, but many things we create by the choices we make. We all come to Earth with a blueprint of our lives. There are certain people we have karma to experience with or complete, lessons to learn, choices to make that develop our moral character.

"I Saw Him Across a Crowded Room and Knew I Would Marry Him!"

Do you know people who have had that experience? I recently interviewed Kelly Ripa and her husband, Mark Consuelos, on my vid/podcast, *CharVision*. Kelly knew the day she was introduced to Mark that he would be her husband. It was an all-knowing feeling of confidence and belonging. It's a familiarity with another person, a complete feeling that is like finding the missing piece of a puzzle and fitting it in. That is not to say that we only have one person we connect with; you can have more than one "soul mate" and "soul mates" who are not romantic. I have friends I believe I was destined to have, and of course, I feel destined to have met my teacher. A soul mate is someone who helps your soul to grow. Like the mythological wizard Merlin, we all have an ability to "remember the future."

Imagination and Dreams

As all of us live in the physical world, we exist and live in the energetic world as well. That's where our imaginations take over. However, intuition and imagination are not that distant from one another. The greatest artists and creative geniuses are fed information. There is a plethora of knowledge in the Universe that is available to all of us. Information is downloaded into us like a computer. Our job is to spell-check and interpret the messages accurately.

To that end, you cannot be wrong in your message. Like I always say, "I'm not always right, but I'm never wrong." I once had a dream that my best friends broke up. They had been together for twelve years. The next day, I told them about my dream. We all laughed about how ridiculous my dream was, until six months later, when they broke up.

We get a lot of our visions in our dreams. Our minds are so busy during the day that sometimes the only time a message can be given to us is when we are asleep. Some dreams are psychic, some are psychological, and some are imaginative thoughts either from what happens during our daily lives or new random experiences that only take place in our dreams.

How vulnerable are you? Did you know that messages can be given to you from different energies, good and bad? That's why I am constantly encouraging my clients, family, and friends to say a prayer of protection. I have had some people tell me they don't believe in prayer. I tell them that prayer is just positive thinking into the Universe. Positive energy attracts positive energy and creates positive results. Unfortunately, negative energy attracts negative energy and creates negative results. That's why it's so important to keep our thoughts positive and not wish bad things on others no matter how horrible they are!

~~~~~~~~~~~~~~~~~~~~~~~~~~~~~~~~~

I always say a prayer of protection before every reading. Put yourself in a white light. Keep all the goodness and love around you. Then put yourself in an egg. The outside of the egg is a mirror. It will send anything negative away from you.

Here is an example psychic prayer of protection you can use:

We ask the universal consciousness and God that holds the highest spiritual power of knowledge, wisdom, and truth to guide and protect us as we communicate with our guides and angels in the spirit world and tap into the wisdom of the Universe. We respect this opportunity and take full responsibility to use this not for ego or controlling others but with the pure intention of spreading love and healing life on this Earth and beyond.

Anything that is in, near, around, or about me that is not of light, go back to where you came from and turn to light if you choose—*but stay away from me!*

When you go on an airplane, they tell you to put your own oxygen mask on before helping the person next to you with theirs. It's the same with protection.

You can also put your loved ones in a white light and mirrored eggs. The first true love is self-love; it means your needs matter. So always protect yourself first, then put your loved ones in their own protective armor of a mirrored egg.

~~~~~~~~~~~~~~~~~~~~~~~~~~~~~~~~~

Blessings in Disguise

What goes around comes around. Karma happens, and the Universe will take care of that energy. Again, to have faith in our whole beings makes life much more comforting. However, it doesn't work unless it is real. It encompasses our bodies, minds, spirits, and souls. It empowers us!

Have you noticed that some of our biggest disappointments turn out to be some of our biggest blessings? My best friend Stuart worked for a big studio in Hollywood for seven years. In 2019, four months before the pandemic, the studio decided to eliminate his and other jobs, since they were looking for places to save money. He received a very handsome severance in his departure, a golden parachute. He would get his fine salary for a whole year.

Then COVID-19 hit! He got to spend quality time with his seventeen-year-old Chihuahua, his constant companion, who was going blind. The day before her eighteenth birthday, she jumped off a chair and broke her jaw. In quarantine, he had to make that terrible decision to send her to heaven. In the early morning of her eighteenth birthday, he drove her to the vet to take her out of her pain. She was a special dog whom we loved very much!

The silver lining regarding work is that he landed an amazing job with a big network a week later. He is constantly getting offers and choosing which projects he wants to work on. I'm telling you this story because when one door closes, another door or window opens a little further down the road. My friend has great faith, and I feel that when we do carry that faith within us, it helps manifest our next opportunity in our lives. Doubt can be a roadblock. Keep the endless possibilities alive in your heart!

What does this have to do with following your intuition and knowing you are psychic? Everything!

There's an old saying: "We make plans, and God laughs." There is always a reason why things happen to educate our souls. Although we find disappointment, there is an opportunity to learn and grow and elevate our souls. Can you think of experiences you have had that were devastating at the time but turned out to bring you joy? Some things are indeed blessings in disguise.

Say you have a dream and your deceased grandmother visits you in it. She's in the kitchen cooking like she always did, but this time the food is burned. It startles you, and you sit up in bed, awakened from your sleep. Is this a message from beyond? What can this mean? This is where we have to interpret it carefully.

The dream you had felt real! You knew it was your grandmother, but she wasn't exactly how you remembered her; however, you felt the familiar feeling of love toward you that only she knew how to show. What does the burned food mean? Usually, the answer will be the first thought that runs through your mind. But sometimes a meaning dawns on you later on when you aren't trying so hard to figure it out. It could mean that something you are preparing in your world needs more attention and you need to be careful that you don't sabotage or ruin it. Try not to destroy it. It could also mean that you should be careful cooking so you literally don't burn yourself. Eventually, you will figure it out. Many messages come like puzzle pieces. They can be symbolic. You may dream about your dog, but it could be a message for someone close to you about *their* dog.

Have you ever been obsessed with an idea or thought and you just can't let it go? My friends and family will tell me that when I get an intuitive or psychic feeling, I'm like a dog with a bone, repeating myself over and over again. I can't let it go. In

2019, I kept seeing 9–11. I would look at the clock, and it would light up 9:11. My guides were trying to tell me something, but I wasn't sure what it was. Could it have been another terrorist attack? No, I didn't think it was that, even though I felt it would happen again. This was different. I kept asking myself what it meant. Maybe it was an attack on human life of another sort. I didn't know what it was, but I knew it would change the way we lived our lives. It would change life as we knew it. I'm sure it was my angels and guides warning me about the pandemic.

I remember on New Year's Eve I was with some friends, and people all over the world were saying they were so happy to be getting rid of life in 2019! How many of us would take that back? Those were the good ol' days. We were free to travel, go to dinner, the theater, movies, concerts, Disney World, and all the fun places we loved to go, without worrying about wearing a mask or contracting a deadly virus.

Perhaps you had a premonition, maybe not about the virus but about something bad happening. I'm sure there are some of you who had warnings in some way or another.

It's important to understand that information is constantly being fed to us from the Universe. I have heard stories where two different musicians from different parts of the world have written almost identical tunes at the same time without even knowing each other.

Many times when I am doing a reading for someone, I'm just validating something that they knew to be true for themselves, because we are all guided. As you will hear me say again and again in this book, I believe there is a blueprint of our lives when we are born, but I also believe that **we create our own destiny through our choices.** Sometimes, our spirit guides step in and decide a future outcome for us. Seth MacFarlane, the creator of *Family Guy*, was scheduled to be on American

Airlines Flight 11, which crashed into the World Trade Center on September 11, 2001. He missed his flight by a few minutes, however, after a night of heavy drinking and after his travel agent mixed up his times. He is grateful to his night out and to the travel agent that screwed up his flight.

Mark Wahlberg was also booked on Flight 11, but he changed his flight a few days earlier because a friend had asked him to fly up to Toronto to watch his film at the Toronto Film Festival. Both men were diverted by divine intervention. This could happen to anyone. "There but for the grace of God, go I."

I have heard stories of angels taking over the steering wheel and preventing a car accident. So sometimes we are being guided and not aware of it because our angels make our decisions for us. Those same helpers who make sure we are in the right place at the right time are also downloading information of wisdom to us to help avoid problems and attain goals in our lives. We live in a physical world, and we live in an energetic world. It is our responsibility to be aware of the energy around us in both.

Children and Intuition

You know who has no filter of divine information? Most children. I keep bringing up sayings most of us have heard before. Many of these sayings are old and often repeated because they are true, such as: "Out of the mouths of babes."

Two through eight can be very profound ages, and during this time, children can share information unintentionally. When my great-nephew was still in a car seat, his parents were driving around looking to buy a home. He was sound asleep in the back seat. They drove up to a house. He woke up for a minute and said, "This is the one," then fell back to sleep. After looking tirelessly for a home, the one he pointed out was the one they bought.

Information is available to all of us when we tap into it. Remember the friend you met as a child and you just knew you would be lifelong friends? This is another example of a soul mate and another example of trusting your intuition before you were old enough to question it.

Everyday Intuition, Signs, and Symbols

Sometimes other people in our lives validate information that we need to know. It could be your spouse, child, or best friend. You may feel that you need an X-ray, or a 3D mammogram. Your sister says, "I just got a 3D mammogram, and I think you should get one, too." It turns out the doctors find something that needs attention.

Have you ever been driving and you think, *I'd better slow down and go the speed limit*? Ten minutes later, you get distracted by a phone call or listening to the radio. You don't realize that you are speeding. The next thing you know, the police lights are flashing in your rearview mirror. The thought came to you for a reason. The Universe always tips us off when we listen!

Another way the Universe can tip you off, as I wrote earlier, is through different signs. You may need an answer to a question like, "Will I get a raise?" You drive by a billboard that says THINGS ARE LOOKING UP. Well, there's your answer. When I was in the Netherlands doing my prime-time show, wondering if it would be successful that season, I always saw the same letters on the license plate from the car in front of me. To this day, whenever I am working on a project, those same letters show up on license plates while I'm driving. It is a sign from the Universe that success is on the way. I'm sure people won't believe me if I told them my spirit guides speak to me through license plate numbers, but the Universe and our guides and angels develop a language of signs with us that only we understand. I spent a lot of time in my car, so to me, it makes sense.

The more those signs appear, the more we understand what they are expressing and communicating to us. It's no different from when we teach our dogs hand signals. The more we guide them, the more we repeat and learn new signs, the more we understand each other. Your guides and angels will be repetitive in their signals to you, and in time, you will understand.

For instance, when I see a rainbow, that means good luck is on the way. It would be great if all signs were positive signs, but some are warnings. Every time I see a dead bird, it means someone I know or who is close to me or a well-known person is going to pass away in the coming months. In fact, that just happened. I kept telling my sister, "They are warning me that someone is going to cross over." A few months later, my assistant of ten years passed away. She was thirty-six years old and died of a massive heart attack.

They try to prepare us psychologically to accept what is ahead. I generally don't predict the deaths of specific people in my readings. I don't usually know who the sign is for when I am tipped off. However, in the '80s, I was on a local television show in Cleveland, Ohio. It was being taped at Cedar Point. The television station sent a limo for me. My father had just had a stroke. As I sat in the back of the limo, I knew that the next time I was going to be in a limo was at my father's funeral. I had never had a feeling like that before. It really upset me to think this. Our father was a wise, kind, loving man, and I adored him! When we get warnings, it affects our emotional state. It's difficult to be objective intuitively and psychically sometimes because there are times we don't want to see or accept what is being given to us. Two weeks later, I was in a limousine at my father's funeral. My guides were trying to prepare me.

Have you ever made a statement and thought, *Where did that come from?* It's like you blurt out a statement and perhaps don't agree with what you said. That has happened to me more than once.

For example, I once was talking to someone who worked for me and found myself saying out loud, "Maybe it's time for you to move on." It surprised both of us when I said it. It was someone who was running my office, and at the time, I thought they were doing a good job. They had convinced me that they were taking care of business, so I didn't let them go.

A year and a half later, I found out that they were not taking care of the office as they were saying. My guides and angels knew there was a problem before I did. That's why when I said the words *maybe it's time for you to move on*, I should have followed through and listened to my gut speaking. I let my trust in them and my emotions of not wanting to let them go get the better of me. Needless to say, they are gone now, but a lot of unpleasantness could have been prevented. There's more to this story that I will share later on.

Sometimes the best thing to do to protect yourself isn't the most convenient or ideal thing to do in the moment but in hindsight would have been the wisest choice to make. **Life is all about the lessons, and as most of us will say, the hardest lessons are the ones we learn the most from.**

I've been teaching others how to get in touch with their psychic intuition for many years now. Some of my students absolutely amaze me! Everyone has their own gifts and excels in different ways. This includes you!

One of my students is definitely a medical intuitive. She is also a nurse by trade. She told a friend that she felt the friend had cancer and it was urgent. My student also felt that her friend would cross over in the near future. At first, the woman and her husband did not pay attention to what my student said. Eventually, this woman ended up going to the doctor, and six weeks later, she died. Not only was my student accurate, she also told this woman the type of cancer it was!

This reminds me of the time a lady came for a reading. All she wanted to know was whether her husband was cheating on her. Which he was . . . but I kept focusing on her health. I was concerned about her or her sister having breast cancer. I kept seeing a lump in the breast. She went for a mammogram. When she got the results, she called me and was agitated that I had suggested to keep an eye on this and get it checked out. It inconvenienced her to get the mammogram. She made sure to call me to let me know I was wrong. I was pleasant and told her I was happy that the results were fine. Six months later, however, she did find a lump in her breast and had to have a mastectomy.

I have another student who, before she ever started working with me, was getting her eyebrows tattooed. As the girl was working on her, my student had a vision of an older man giving her money. She told the artist what she saw. The woman began crying. She said, "That is my stepfather! He recently passed away and left me money so I could open this shop with my daughter!" When my student told me this story, I wasn't surprised, because she is gifted. I also encouraged her that next time she has a vision to ask the person if it is okay to share it. It is courteous to ask first, and in my opinion, the only way to share psychic information is with permission. Many people don't want to be given information that they are not asking for.

They feel attacked. Also, you don't know if people are open to the subject. This student is definitely a medium and a psychic. Whenever I get a message for someone at random, not in a reading, I ask permission before sharing it.

The student I am referring to is many years younger than I am—she is a millennial. I find it fascinating because the veil between our everyday lives and the energetic world is thinner for her. I find that many younger people have been born with an intuition and psychic ability that it took years for me to break through; I credit the parents who raised this generation for being more open and accepting. In addition to being brilliant, she is open to signs; while my spirit guides speak to me through things like license plates, she gets emojis from her guides! When she told me this, I smiled. She was born into a technological age, and emojis would be a familiar sign for her to identify with.

Our guides and the Universe communicate with us through symbols that we are familiar with and understand. It's like learning to read and interpret another language.

I have another student who is also a nurse and has worked in hospice care. She helps the terminally ill cross over. She told me about how people start talking to their loved ones on the other side before they cross over. They see their beloved mother or father or grandparent beckoning them to come with them. Later on in this book, I will talk about people who have had near-death experiences and have come back to life and shared what it was like.

Famous celebrities either knowingly or unknowingly have predicted their own deaths. The Notorious B.I.G., Christopher Wallace, was one of the biggest rap icons of our time. He was a prominent figure in the East Coast–West Coast rivalry. He liked to disrespect Tupac Shakur in his music. In his song "Suicidal Thoughts," B.I.G. confesses that he hears death calling to him. Although he alluded to dying in a few songs he wrote, these lyrics stand out because they're from the very last song on his very last album, titled *Ready to Die.* He was killed by an unknown assailant in a Los Angeles drive-by shooting. Speaking of Tupac Shakur, who lived his whole life surrounded by gangs and violence, it may have been obvious to some in his song "N-ggas Done Changed," which was released two months after his death. In it he predicts being shot and murdered.

Mark Twain, long considered the father of American literature, with his classics *Tom Sawyer* and *Huckleberry Finn,* accurately predicted the exact day of his death. Twain was born in 1835 shortly after a celestial visit from Halley's Comet. He would later joke that the next time it came, he would "go with it." The author believed that God must have said, "Now here are these two unaccountable freaks; they came in together, they must go out together." When the comet returned in 1910, Twain made true on his prediction and died of a heart attack the day after its passing.

I recently had a seven-year-old boy on *CharVision,* my vid/podcast. His grandmother used to watch me on local television in Detroit on *Kelly and Company.* She called to get help and guidance for her grandson. His name is Sage. He is adorable! He told me about his great-grandfather's spirit coming to visit him and how loved and protected he felt. His ability to see spirits is remarkable. He had a visitation from Rev. Martin Luther King. Sage loves history and knew exactly who he was. We also had a very adult conversation about Black Lives Matter and civil rights. I began the interview teaching him how to pray and protect himself with the white light and mirrored egg. I have shared that powerful protection process with you in this book as well.

His grandmother had told me that he doesn't always see positive energies. On one occasion, Sage saw the grim reaper. That really infuriated me. As I always say, as in everyday life, there are good and bad people, in the spirit world, there are positive and negative energies. It could have also been a dark spirit portraying the grim reaper. Nevertheless, that kind of energy is not welcome around the pure and innocent! Remember: **we control spirits, they don't control us, unless we give them the power to do so!** I feel confident that Sage understands how to protect himself, based on what I taught him. After he saw the grim reaper, he told me his dad read some poems to him from a book. His mother told me that it was his dad reading to him from the Bible, and they prayed to Jesus. That was comforting. I am a big believer in the protective power of prayer.

Just as my parents listened to me when I was younger and knew among other things when those people overcharged us, Sage's parents understand that he has an ability to connect to the spirit world and obtain information. This work is not a toy. It is most important to respect the process with an open mind but with a protective energy.

When I first started studying and developing my psychic abilities, I was a substitute schoolteacher. I was only twenty-one years old. It turned out that I was a popular substitute. One day, I was covering a study hall. I was reading a book and not looking at the students. The class seemed to be well-behaved until one girl shouted, "Someone took my shoe!" I lifted my head, looked right at a young man, and said, "Michael, give her the shoe back!" There were thirty-five students in the class. Logically, I had no idea who had taken her shoe. However, my psychic ability came to the rescue. It just flowed out of my mouth. That's how our intuitive abilities work much of the time. We randomly get a feeling and just go with it!

All the previous examples illustrate how our psychic abilities are natural, in all of us, and how we sometimes experience them without even realizing what they are.

Below are my Psychic Main Points and some ways to practice in your psychic journal.

Psychic Main Points

* You are already psychic.
* The Universe is always trying to speak to you—through your gut feelings, your nagging thoughts, dreams, your imagination, signs, and symbols.
* The Universe will always tip you off about evil.
* We can have these intuitive thoughts for ourselves and for others.
* Make sure to use the psychic prayer of protection each day and before doing any psychic work. You can use the one I put in this chapter, or you can write your own prayer, based on your intuition.
* It's important to listen to your intuition. Add your reason to what your message conveys in your Psychic Journal Practice.
* Have you ever said something that came out of your mouth that you didn't mean to say? You realized you didn't mean to say it. Your emotions got in the way and you dismissed it. Later you will find out that the Universe was tipping you off about something to protect you. Listen!

Psychic Journal Practice

Write on the front of your journal/notebook: *I AM PSYCHIC.*
Declare it, believe it, know it.

If you haven't already, answer the questions I asked at the beginning of the chapter.

Answer these questions:

* What resonated with you in this chapter? Why?
* How would you like intuition to help you in your life?
* What excites you about developing your psychic abilities?
* What frightens you about developing your psychic abilities?

2

THE ENERGY THUMBPRINT

What you will learn in this chapter: Energy is all around us and in us. In fact, everything is energy. Therefore, energy can be felt and experienced, and our lives themselves are energy. Energy doesn't just disappear; it leaves thumbprints in time that we can connect with. And energy can also give us intuitive prompts to keep us connected.

Our thoughts are extremely powerful. Thoughts are things. Thoughts create reality. Thoughts are the vehicle used to hear the messages from loved ones in the spirit world and from the universal knowledge of goodness, love, and wisdom. Our thoughts create the energy we experience.

We need to be aware of our thoughts. **Positive thoughts attract more positive thoughts and create positive results.** Unfortunately, negative thoughts attract more negative thoughts and create negative results. Those people who live in constant fear will not understand when their intuition is trying to guide them. Why? Because their fear thoughts are creating more fear thoughts and a fearful experience.

You might think that you are at the mercy of your thoughts. But did you know that you can choose your own thoughts? You can choose your thoughts, which then determine your perception, which then determines your experience. Two people can have similar situations but see the situations completely differently. What's the difference? To a large extent, it's how we choose to see the situation, which all begins with our thoughts, which in turn affect our attitude.

Another example of how our thoughts create the energy we live from is this: Have you ever heard the saying "You're only as old as you feel"? That speaks to this. Two people can be the same age, and one chooses thoughts like, *Getting old is difficult,* and spends a lot of time remembering past memories and regrets. Another person, the same age, can choose thoughts like, *Every day, in every way, my life improves!* and *The older the grape, the sweeter the wine,* and is always looking forward to new opportunities.

Have you been around a person who has negative energy? You can feel it from them: their conversations are negative, their demeanor is sour, and when you are around them, you end up feeling drained and negative yourself. That's your gut feeling letting you know this person is not good to spend a lot of time with. But the reverse is also true. Have you been around someone who is positive and happy, and seems to have a joyful outlook on life, even during the difficult times? When you are around them, you feel energized and happier. Which kind of person do you surround yourself with? Which kind of person are you?

It all begins with our thoughts, which affect our energy.

A good exercise is to make a list of your thoughts during the day. Make a column of positive thoughts, and then make a list of negative thoughts. (Don't worry, I'll remind you again to do this at the end of the chapter!) If you are living in constant fear or negativity, the Universe doesn't have an opportunity to tip you off to stay out of harm's way.

CHAR TIP: POSITIVE THOUGHTS, POSITIVE ENERGY

You have probably heard of affirmations. Affirmations are positive statements that we make, fed into our subconscious minds to help us create a more focused, positive reality. There isn't anything magical about them; they are just ways to "wire" ourselves in a particular way. In one sense, all thoughts we have are affirmations, in that they affirm the reality we are choosing to see. So it's important to choose as many positive thoughts as we can—affirmations are thoughts we choose consciously.

The key with affirmations is to make them positive, in the present moment, and declare something that we want to become true. The following are some positive affirmations:

* I am in harmony with life, and all is good in my world.
* I am always in the right place, at the right time, surrounded by the right people.
* I am in control of my thoughts, and I choose to love my life.
* I am positive, happy, and successful.
* I own my power.
* I have a positive attitude.
* I am grateful. I practice gratitude.

Now, write some of your own. Perhaps you can look at that list of negative thoughts you wrote during the earlier exercise. Write a positive affirmation to counter the negative thoughts.

The more you repeat the positive affirmations, the more you will experience their results. And if you are able to state them out loud, that makes it even realer for you.

What does this have to do with being psychic? As I've stated, when we connect to positive energy, we are able to be more positive and to create more positive results. Positive affirmations plug you into positive energy in the Universe, which means that your psychic connection will be more positive.

~~~~~~~~~~

THE F-WORD

I call *fear* the four-letter f-word: false evidence appearing real. **You will never develop your psychic intuition with an attitude of fear or negativity. The answer is to live with faith and hope.** Knowing you are protected and guided brings a sense of calm and stability. When we are emotionally, psychologically, and physically balanced, we are able to receive and send messages with a sense of knowing. Owning your power makes you a much stronger intuitive.

It is essential to own your power when tuning in. When you are balanced, if you have a thought that a person or situation isn't to be trusted, I urge you to listen and to avoid this person or situation at all costs—it will be clear to you. However, if you do tune in to something that is fantastic and feels right, go for it! Embrace it and be grateful for it.

Let me add a bit of warning here: this is where some people allow their egos to get in the way. They see this guidance as something that comes from themselves, and this feeds their egos. As I mentioned, ego means "edging God out." When you are a secure person and use your ability with compassion and empathy, there is no need to feed your ego. If your intent to use this ability is about helping others and really owning that desire, your intuitive psychic gifts will expand. However, if you are using this to control or con others, not only will it bring you bad karma, the powers that be will do their best to remove you from those you are taking advantage of. And when I say *remove*, I mean get rid of you in some way.

CHAR TIP: A SIMPLE TUNING-IN PRACTICE

First, find a quiet spot where you can take a couple of minutes uninterrupted. Put down your phone and anything else that can distract you. Don't worry, this is only for a couple of minutes— you can have your toys back soon! I will reiterate how to protect yourself more than once in this book.

Imagine yourself in a blinding white light, so bright that if anyone looks at you, their eyes will have to be protected. Then put yourself in a mirrored egg and close it up. The love and protection is inside the egg with you. The outer shell of the egg is a mirror, so anything that is evil will reflect back to where it came from. You will then say the prayer that I shared previously.

Second, you can do this standing or sitting, but if you have the option, sit down. Plant your feet on the floor and close your eyes. Take a deep breath in and hold it for a count of four, and then release it for a count of four. Do that two or three more times. Breathing intentionally relaxes us and helps us to focus.

Third, take in the breaths again, but this time on the inhale count, silently say, *I am here now.* And on the exhale count, silently say, *I release and let go.* Do this three or four times at least. You can do this for as long as it helps you. (By the way—one bonus Char Tip—you can do this just about anywhere where it is safe to do so—your home, an elevator, your office, walking down the street, and so on. Obviously, in those situations, your eyes will be open, and you won't be handling any machinery or anything. But those two statements place you firmly in the present moment and help you to lower anxiety, fear, anger, or any other negative emotion.)

You can end at the third step, but if you are interested, you can go one step further.

This fourth step is another way of using your tuned-in energy to receive psychic messages. Ask yourself the following question, and don't judge the responses that pop up:

Is there anything I need to know right now?

Just ask and see if any thoughts come. Let your mind go blank, and trust the first thought that comes to you. Don't push or force anything. Do not allow your desires to get in the way of the message, unless of course the answer is a good one! And if nothing comes up, that's okay, too—that's also an answer of sorts! If something comes up, think about it and, if positive, act on it. The Universe will give you the answer eventually, and you will know it when it happens.

~~~~~~~~~~~~~~~~~

I write my books mostly to help you understand your own intuition to help your life and the lives of those in your circle, not necessarily so you can hang a shingle and begin a career of being a psychic reader for hire. In truth, very few people are really destined to take this to that level. Some people think they have a gift but are not always aware of the source from which they are receiving their messages. The trickster energies fool them. So they are like walking Ouija boards; they will tell you nine great things, and then the tenth thing they will tell you could be very dangerous and destructive. I only use that as an example, because the Ouija board is marketed as a toy for children. The problem is that it brings forth very low-level entities and usually evil energies. I don't like Ouija boards, and I don't like anything that makes light of the spirit world, crossing over, or bad energies; I suggest you stay far away from them. If I sound like a broken record, it's because I want this to come across: again, the world runs like a battery. There is always a positive and a negative charge. (And yes, I'll probably repeat that again a few more times before we're done in the book!)

One time when I was in New York City on business, I was waiting in the lobby of a high-rise hotel at an elevator bank. I had pressed the button to go up. I noticed there was a man next to me, and I could feel a strong wave of negative, dark, weird energy coming from him. When the elevator doors opened, I foolishly went into the elevator with him. He pressed twelve, and I pressed fourteen. Strangely, when we reached the twelfth floor, the man didn't get off. The doors closed, and he was still in the elevator with me. When the floor stopped at the four-teenth floor, I got off the elevator, and so did he. This time, I listened to my intuition about his energy. I saw that the doors of another elevator on the fourteenth floor were also opening, and that elevator was going down. I immediately jumped into the next elevator and went back to the lobby. This all happened so quickly that it must have caught him off guard, and he wasn't able to make it onto that elevator.

As soon as I got to the lobby, I left the building for a while. Later, when I returned, he was nowhere to be seen. I went to my floor and my room and was safe. I'm sure he was going to follow me on the fourteenth floor, and I'm also certain that by tuning in to his energy and taking action, I avoided a big issue and problem. That's what's so great about listening to your guidance, but had I truly been listening, I never would have entered the elevator in the first place.

See, this is what I mean about "energy." You can use it in big and small ways. You can avoid disasters in your life. You can also obtain the goals you want to achieve. Here's a story about feeling the energy, and then taking action, and seeing what that led to.

Energy in Action

One time, when I was tuning in and paying attention to the energy around and in me, I had a feeling to contact my dear friend Joanne Saltzman. This was right after Kathy Gifford had left *Live with Regis*, and Joanne was the talent booker on the show. Years before, Joanne and I had become friends when she was a producer for a local talk show in Boston, Massachusetts. At that time, she had wanted to book me for *Good Day Boston*. I asked, "Are you going to book me without me reading for you?" I always read for the producers when they book me, because I don't want anyone to have me on the show who doesn't believe in my gift. I want to make sure I am always honoring the spirit guides who honor me with their guidance. Joanne was the first producer who really didn't care if she had a reading. It wasn't about believing or not believing; she just had a job to do. I read for her anyway, and we are close friends to this day.

So fast-forward to autumn in about 2000, when I contacted her because my tuned-in energy said to check in with her. She told me it was a good time to call, because they were auditioning people for the show, and she would love to book me. After some back-and-forth about timing, Joanne suggested I go on the air in November. That sounded fine to me! Since Kathy Lee had left, they were auditioning new cohosts for Regis. Kelly Ripa, an actress from the soap opera *All My Children*, was cohosting on the day I was booked. Michael Gelman, the producer, asked me to read for her, and I never say no to Gelman!

Now, a side note that ties in to the story. A few weeks earlier, I had been to Italy with my friend who was helping me share my work on TV in Germany, Spain, and the Netherlands. While in Florence, Italy, at the Duomo Cathedral, I asked the woman in the gift shop if there was a patron saint of television. She said it was Saint Clare. So being the good Jew that I am, I bought a wooden Saint Clare statuette.

Okay, back to my appearance on Regis's show. As I was getting ready for the show, I slipped the little wooden piece in my pocket for good luck. Sometimes objects like that are good reminders to stay focused and tuned in to the positive energy of the Universe.

I had never met Kelly Ripa before. When we were standing there on set, the cameras rolling, I tuned in to her energy. Suddenly, I felt the presence of a woman in the spirit realm standing next to Kelly. I asked if she had someone deceased with an *E* initial. I said, "Like Esther?" I also told her that I saw a *D*. Kelly looked at me, stunned. It was true, she had lost a loved one named Esther. Then I said that Esther was holding a baby and blurted out the first thing I felt: "You're not pregnant yet, are you?"

She gasped. Regis said, "Excuse me, are you expecting?" She said, "I haven't told my boss yet!"

Then I said, "Oh my God!" I hugged her and congratulated her. It actually was one of those magical television moments that don't happen often. Whenever I see her now, she reminds me that she believed me once I mentioned the initial *D*. Why? They called this person Esther *Dee*!

Recently, when Kelly and her husband, Mark Consuelos, were on my vid/podcast, *CharVision*, Mark told me he was at home watching that day and almost fell over because they were the only ones who knew she was pregnant! He then told me at that time he was a little afraid of me! The *Regis* clip has been shown on different TV shows hundreds of times. It was also voted the audience favorite that year. Although I had a feeling to call to be on the show that autumn, it was Joanne Saltzman who insisted on me being on in November the day Kelly Ripa was going to be on. I am grateful to her and to Kelly, Regis, Ryan Seacrest, and Gelman for their support of my work through the years.

Imagine if I had not tuned in to my energy that day. Imagine if I had had the impulse to call my old friend, but didn't do it. I hope this story shows you that a) it's important to tune in and listen, and b) take action on any positive suggestion. You don't know where it will lead!

Variety magazine just named that segment one of the top ten talk show guest appearances in television talk show history! It is known in pop culture as the gift that keeps giving.

Energy Thumbprint

We all have our own unique energy thumbprints. Have you ever had a house full of people and your back is to the door and someone walks in the room? Perhaps you are doing the dishes or on your computer. You can't see them, but you instinctively feel their energy. It's a familiar, all-knowing feeling. You even know if it's your sister, your brother, your child, your spouse, or your friend. That's because we all have a unique energy that is specifically our very own.

This energy thumbprint carries us through eternity. People ask me, "Well, if someone dies, how can they come back and communicate with us if we are reincarnated?" The answer is that whenever we live a lifetime, our spirits go to our souls. Our souls are made up of every person and spirit we were from past lifetimes. After our deaths, we go to the other side and judge ourselves in God's eyes.

Were we kind and compassionate?

Did we leave any stones unturned with our loved ones or other souls?

The Universe recycles us into another being, and a part of us becomes a new spirit. Let's say you were a caveman and you hit your wife over the head with a club, you let your kids stay hungry, and you really didn't do a very good job as a human. When you die, you judge yourself, and because the goal is to elevate our souls in each lifetime, you are reincarnated into another being to do better the next life. Maybe this time you are a woman with children and your husband crosses over and you have to support your family alone. Maybe you are abusive to your children or have no patience.

When you cross over, you judge yourself, and you are aware you did a little better than the previous lifetime but still had a lot to learn. So in the next life, you are a monk, you live your life in prayer, but still have bitterness and anger in your heart. You still haven't learned all your life's lessons. That caveman, that mother, and that monk are recycled in your soul, and new people keep coming out to learn life's lessons to elevate your soul until you sit at the right hand of God, the highest form of goodness and love, so that you become one with the highest energy that exists. Then you are ready to use your energy to heal and help the Universe.

So to answer the question, that caveman, that mother, and that monk each have their own unique energy thumbprints that exist always. That's why your mother or father who passed away twenty years ago can come into a reading and help you with your life. **Time does not exist on the other side. An hour is no different from a week or a year—or a lifetime.**

I've had clients say, "Well, I hardly knew my grandmother. Why is she here?" I say, "Without your grandmother, you wouldn't exist." Some people try to be so technical about their readings and try to produce them. The information from a reading comes *through* me, not *from* me. I have no control over who shows up.

This is why it is important to increase your energy thumbprint through your thoughts and your actions. The more you learn in this life, the closer you are to healing yourself and the Universe. This book can help you take a big step forward in increasing your energy thumbprint. Doing the exercises and absorbing the information will increase your sensitivity to energy, both within and all around you.

CHAR TIP:
PAST LIVES

Get your I AM PSYCHIC Journal and do the following exercise. As you do it, you might begin to have doubts or feel excited, or maybe nothing will come up at all. Any response is okay; this is just a light exploration.

First, find a quiet area where you won't be interrupted. Sit down and relax.

Second, take a few deep breaths. (You can use the breathing technique we discussed in the tuning-in exercise from earlier in this chapter.)

Third, ask yourself this: "If I have lived lives before, what were they? What were my previous lives?" Look down at your feet. This is one thing people often see first when seeing who they were in a past life. Then look at your clothes and then your surroundings. Ask what year it is. What is your gender identity? How old are you? Your response will come like automatic writing. The pen will take to paper and start flowing with thoughts and experiences.

Fourth, record any thoughts that come up. Don't judge what you write, just record what thoughts come to mind. If a previous incarnation that you lived comes up in your mind, write it down, with any qualities that come with it. (For example: *Young woman, 1700s, China, happy but felt lonely,* etc.)

If more than one entity presents itself to you, write those down as well.

I'm not here to convince you if these were "real" or not, but I do think that since your mind brought them forward, you might have something you can learn from them. Perhaps they are pointing you to something you need to examine in this lifetime.

You will also remember people in your past lives who you know now, although the relationships may be different (e.g., your husband may have been your father, or your child may have been your parent).

Energy Thumbprint, Not Google!

I first started doing psychic readings long before social media or Google. In the 1980s, I did a pilot for a TV show and read for the audience that I spoke about earlier. I was so accurate that a newscaster in Canada accused me of having researchers bring me information. Now, on a rare occasion, I get a wacky person who accuses me of googling them! Those people are connected to the trickster energies that will try to sabotage someone's hope of connecting with their loved one again.

The internet and Google didn't even exist for many years of my work. I don't google people, I use my psychic skills to tune in to someone's energy thumbprint. Sometimes people refuse to believe it. A while ago, a man called to book a reading. Normally, people leave messages or talk to my assistant, but in this case, I personally answered the phone. I immediately felt a connection with him, and instead of booking him for a reading months down the road, I felt a desperate energy trying to get through to him. I instantly knew it was his son. Losing a child has to be the most difficult loss someone can have.

I asked the man if I could ask him a question. He said yes. I said, "Did you lose your son? I feel him here." I told him his son's name and mentioned the baseball cap the son was wearing that had the logo of his favorite team. The father said his son had indeed passed and that was the cap he had been wearing when he died.

I was so excited for the spirit of the son and the father to reconnect that I did not charge him. The father was grateful, and we hung up, both feeling inspired by the reading.

Soon after, I received an email from the father, accusing me of googling him! I was dumbfounded. I mean, I had literally just picked up the phone and had no idea who this person was! I was able to tell him about his son within seconds. I felt bad for the son on the other side. The father was a lost soul and had no hope or faith, and this young spirit had appeared to try to help his father.

There are those people in the world who don't have faith. It's easy and tempting to blame others for our losses, and it's tempting to blame God. Terrible things happen, and we want to blame someone. It's only natural. Blame and anger are important steps in our healing process, especially anger; the key, however, is to do whatever work you can, as hard as it is to work past that and get to the point where you can heal. As much as we miss those who crossed over, we need to make room for the living.

Feeling and Following the Energy

I have three students at the moment who are real estate agents. When Sally knows a house is the right one for her clients, she gets a tingling sensation in her feet as soon as she walks in the door. There is no doubt. She just knows it is the right one for the client!

Everyone has their own language with their intuition and their spirit guides. The spirits usually show us things in symbols. Sometimes it's just an all-knowing feeling. My car kept breaking, so I decided to get a new one. My friend had a Range Rover. When I saw his car, I had a feeling that I should get a Land Rover, a car made in England. I was in Los Angeles, but I called my longtime friend Bob, who lived in Indiana and owned car dealerships, though they were for American and Japanese cars. It was completely illogical to call him, since the car I knew I should get was British.

But I had a feeling. I told Bob I wanted a pre-owned white Land Rover with a beige interior and low miles. He said, "Char, you know I don't carry that brand, but I will keep my eye out." He has known me long enough to know my "feelings." A week later, he called me. "So my brother-in-law came to visit us with his family from North Carolina. They drove to Indiana. I looked outside my window and saw that he had a white Land Rover. I went to look at it, and it had a beige interior. I asked him if he was interested in selling it. He said, 'Actually, it's for sale! I want to buy a truck.' He gave me the price, and we made a deal! I made arrangements for the car to come to Los Angeles." This was a few years ago. So far so good—the car is great! I never even test-drove it, and I bought it sight unseen. I just knew, and I knew I could trust Bob.

I bought the car because I had a psychic feeling about it, and I followed that prompt. But I don't feel that psychic hit for everything. The funny part is a couple of days after I bought the car, I needed a refrigerator for my home in Michigan. I found one online that seemed like it would fit in the space in my kitchen. I hadn't gotten a psychic hit on that model. I'd had a very busy day, but I still jumped in the car to drive more than an hour to Lowe's to see it, to make sure I liked it. Yep, I spent thousands on a preowned car, sight unseen, but made sure I drove at night in a rainstorm to see my $800 refrigerator!

Saying Yes to Intuitive Actions

I have a friend named Teran Davis, a lovely lady who is very spiritual and intuitive. Every year, Teran hosts an afternoon tea just before Christmas to raise money for underprivileged children. The Los Angeles Fire Department runs the charity. It's a great cause. Everyone brings toys for the children. Teran is a kind, generous host, and the hall is always beautifully decorated. There's a long magical train that has everything you can imagine—small towns with post offices, markets, and figurines of people and animals. The food for the high tea is delicious.

There is always a gift bag at her events—she goes all out! For Christmas in December 2019, the gift bag contained many items, including a beautiful Swarovski pen, some high-end hair products, and . . . a face mask? What? This wasn't any old face mask with a pretty design or a famous logo on it. No, this was a serious one: an N95 face mask. I just couldn't understand why she would include a face mask as a gift, but thought there must be a reason. I recently saw Teran at Paris Hilton's wedding. I told Teran's date how amazing it was that she'd put an N95 mask in the gift bag. She interrupted me and said, "You were the only person who said, 'I think I will really need this.'" Well, what none of us knew is that we would all be desperate to wear this very type of face mask a few months later. In fact, medical officials were saying that all N95 masks were to be worn by medical personnel only. They were nearly impossible to find for quite a while. You have to admit that this was an unusual gift to give. The CDC advises that they are the safest masks. But Teran is so psychically connected that she followed her intuition to give this to us. I'm still blown away that she was guided to put that mask in the gift bag! It goes to show that **when you get an intuitive suggestion, it won't always make sense to you or anyone else. But if it is a positive action, follow it!** Let my friend be an inspiration.

Psychic Main Points

* Everything is energy.
* Our thoughts are energy. Everything we think contributes to our experience.

* Since everything is energy, everything leaves a "thumb-print" behind. Every life leaves an impression in the Universe.
* Life allows us to reincarnate over and over, learning more each time, so that we keep opening ourselves up to higher experiences and healing ourselves and the world.
* One way we can increase our energy thumbprint in the world is to follow our intuitive direction. Follow it even when it doesn't make sense (when it isn't dangerous or negative).

Psychic Journal Practice

Get your I AM PSYCHIC Journal.
Answer these questions:

* What do you feel life is trying to say to you right now?
* What actions can you take that your intuition seems to be encouraging you to take? Are these actions positive?
* What question would you ask your intuition if you could? (Now close your eyes, take a few deep breaths, ask that question, and record the answer!)

As you write, let the words flow using stream of consciousness.

3

LETTING GO

~~~~~~

What you will learn in this chapter: Part of our intuitive practice is learning to let go. If we don't let go, we don't stay open to the energy of life flowing through us. We get stuck. Letting go means letting go of assumptions, unforgiveness, and anything else that keeps us held back. No matter how desperate you are for an answer, or how emotionally invested you are, you literally need to let go and let God. The more emotional we are about it—though there are exceptions— the more we block the truth from floating in our thoughts.

~~~~~~

Saying goodbye to a loved one and letting go is so heart-breaking.

When we know a loved one is suffering, it helps us to let them go. A caller on my podcast shared her story. She said, "I just can't think of getting another dog just yet." I told her I knew how hard it was. We never replace an animal or a person. I know women who get married again right after their husbands die, but it's too heartbreaking to get another dog! The day this caller's dog Runty died, she saw a bird on her roof. Because the bird had blue eye shadow, she thought it could be a "mourning" bird. You know our loved ones in heaven don't want us to be sad. Just like our animals feel our moods and our energy and our sadness, while they are here with us, they feel it there as well. So do our human loved ones. They don't want us to be sad. However, we never replace a person or an animal. I told her about the time I had a visitation from my horse in a dream. I was in a field, and she was next to the only tree in it. She came running to me, I jumped on her bare back, and we galloped around the field. The next morning when I woke up I could smell her on my hands. I explained to her that animals go to an animal heaven. Dogs know unconditional love. That's something we all could learn. There are different neighborhoods over there, but animals are always protected. I can't say the same for all people. They wait until we get there, and then we reunite with them once again. I was thinking, when we are on our deathbeds, how do we make that transition easier? Well, just think about all the loved ones who crossed over before you. Think of the beautiful reunions you will have with them. For those who pass quickly, especially if they are young, it is probably harder for them to realize they have passed on. Those who are terminal patients have more time to think about their passing. For most people, it is a beautiful experience. Hopefully, you have lived an honest life with a clear conscience. Hopefully, when you judge yourself, you can learn from your mistakes, forgive yourself, and move on. That's the time you can work on elevating your soul.

Another caller that night was Sylvia. She had been to two of my intuition retreats with her sister, Barb. She told the story about their 101-year-old aunt whose name was also Sylvia. Her aunt was not really spiritual or into metaphysics. One day in the nursing home where she lived, she was talking to her niece on the phone. She said, "You know, Bill was here! He was here, but I know he is dead!" Bill was her husband. She definitely had a visitation from him, but she was confused, because her logical mind knew that he had passed away years ago. It's helpful that her nieces could explain that this is possible and that loved ones in spirit come to visit us. During our call, I kept seeing feathers. Sylvia said that she had birds but always collected feathers and painted feathers.

Another caller that evening was Mary Ellen. Her stepfather passed away in 2007. He died in a car accident, and there was alcohol involved. Right before he died, Mary Ellen got into a big argument with him. She carried a lot of guilt. When he came to her in a dream, he said, "I thought you would be mad at me," and she said, "I don't even care." She forgave him, and he forgave her. They hugged each other, and it was so real she could feel their embrace. It's always important to forgive so you don't carry that negativity. In some cases, if someone was evil to you, it is okay to forgive but not give your love or energy to that person; however, in this case, there was complete closure.

Mary Ellen also had a visitation from her dad. He'd passed on a Friday, and the following Tuesday, she had the dream. She remembered hugging him and asking if he was okay, and he kept assuring her that he was and not to worry, that everything would be fine. In the dream, it was raining, and they did not want to let each other go. It was so vivid, and she could feel the rain. Her father then said, "It's time to wake up," and so she did.

She also talked about her experience having terrible sleep paralysis. In those instances, she felt like she was asking for help, but no one heard her. She would then surround herself with the white light and the mirrored egg, which she learned about from my book. It really worked for her.

Mary Ellen's call made me remember that when I was very young, I would have sleep paralysis—you cannot move or scream for help; you think it, but you can't express it. I always prayed to God, and it would go away. It does not happen to me anymore. But if it happens to you, ask your divine creator to help you, put yourself in the white light and mirrored egg, and demand that the energy go away. Mary Ellen realized that it was a dark energy trying to influence her. I am so happy for her that she is in control of her energy now!

One time when I was a regular guest on *A.M. LA*, my parents visited me and came to the studio. We took the executive producer, Ron Ziskin, and his wife, Diane, out for dinner in Malibu. Diane asked if anyone else in our family was psychic and saw spirits. I immediately said no. Then my dad interjected, "Yes, I do!"

"What?" I said.

"Yeah, honey," he said. "Your grandma and grandpa come to my bedside all the time and tell me things."

I was shocked! "Daddy, why didn't you ever tell me?"

"Well, I thought people would think I was crazy, but they put you on TV and respect you, so I guess it's okay to talk about it now!"

CHAR TIP: LETTING-GO PRACTICE

We all need to let go. As a psychic intuitive, you will learn that letting go is part of the process, both for ourselves and for helping others. Here is an affirmation that you can use to see letting go not as a loss but rather as a beautiful gesture.

Take a deep breath, surround yourself with white light, think of what (or who) needs to be released, and then say (either out loud or to yourself):

I let go of _____ unconditionally with love, forgiveness, and healing . . . and so it is.

Fill in the blank with what (or who) needs to be released.

Feel free to change that affirmation to fit more closely to your own situation, or write something equally powerful that allows you and everyone whom you are thinking of to move on freely and unencumbered.

Death is also a rebirth. As much as we love and need the person we love who crossed over, it's crucial to let them go on their journey at their pace. Our love and energy can keep them earthbound. We need to be unselfish and wish them well. Put the white light around yourself, then put the white light around them. Then with your thoughts, encourage them to look for the white light of love and God. Find your guardian angels and spirit guides. Let your loved ones go, and tell them you will see them again when it is your turn to cross over and you will reunite once again. Our love is eternal. Enjoy the journey!

We had another caller who had a visitation from a spirit. Orisia has been my client since the early '80s. She recalled how I told her she would adopt a child but it would take longer than she expected. It would turn out great for them. Their daughter is now twenty-one years old and has been a joy in their lives. All Orisia's life, she thought she knew a spirit was there. As a child, there was a place in her house where she felt her grandmother. Every time she went to that place in their home, she would tell her parents that Grandma was right there, and they were like, "Yeah, yeah, yeah." When she was nine, she saw spirits, some of whom she was afraid of. One day, she was in New Mexico getting a massage. The massage therapist said she was also a psychic. Orisia felt someone at the end of the table, by her foot. She saw an old man who looked Native American. Since they were in New Mexico, it made sense to her that it would be a Native American man. She asked the massage therapist if she felt any spirits around them, and she said, "Yes, at the end of the table, next to your right foot." It also turns out that Orisia's daughter sees spirits. On this call, Orisia thanked me for all the good advice over the years. I told her it was my honor. I am so blessed to be reading for some families for over forty years. In fact, in some cases, I'm reading for a third generation—the original client is deceased, and now they are coming back to connect with their children and grandchildren.

Another caller named Lisa gave me encouragement to write this book because I had said earlier in the program that I was procrastinating. She said that Wayne Dyer always believed that books were already written; we just have to download them. He would take an old book and put its cover on the book he was writing, to help manifest the book into reality. My sister Alicia kept encouraging me and also said this book would be guided through me.

Lisa told a story about when she was five years old and would get fevers every week until she got her tonsils out. They had this older house with a long, high staircase. She then added, "I can hear my mom now saying, 'Don't tell people the floating story!'" One night while her parents were in their bed, she had a very high fever, and she remembered clearly that she walked to the top of the stairs. Looking down, she started to kneel, thinking she would go down the stairs like their dog. But all of a sudden, she started floating! She was holding on to the banister. When she got to the bottom of the stairs, she looked in the dining room, and to this day, she doesn't know why she wasn't frightened. There was a man and woman, and they were talking to her about their country. They told her every Christmas they had a yule log cake. Now, this is not her background. She is Irish and Native American and German. Their story is more Scandinavian. They said, "You are young, and you have to get to bed now."

She said, "I'm afraid. Will you walk me to the bottom of the stairs?" She turned back, and the couple was still there. She waved to them, and they waved back. The next thing she knew, she was up in her room, where she saw her physical body and went back into it. She only found out years later about something called a yule log cake. There was no way she could have known about it as a child.

I told her that she'd gone on an astral flight. This is when your ethereal body leaves your physical body. There is a silver thread that connects the spirit body to the physical body. You *never* want that to be severed. You can never be disconnected. I told her about the time I was at my home in Michigan sleeping, and I floated up and out right through the glass window. I have old-fashioned glass windows with wooden panes around the squares of glass. I went through the glass to the outside. I could not feel the temperature. I looked at the forest and then looked back through the window and saw myself sound asleep. It scared me; I didn't look like myself. I jumped back into my physical body. They say we don't really look the way others see us when we see our reflections in a mirror. I now see why.

Lisa then told another story. She had a friend who at a

young age had a terminal blood disease, similar to leukemia. This was her first contemporary who had a serious illness. They gave her friend three years at the most to live. Lisa would visit her, and her friend rallied many times. Lisa is an avid animal lover who has always had a lot of cats. Her friend was an animal lover, too, although not as active as Lisa, who worked rescuing strays and finding homes for them. When her friend became extremely ill, Lisa went to visit her in hospice. Her friend said, "There are cats all over this room. Just before you got here, the room filled up with cats!" Lisa felt it was her friend's guides' way of preparing her that she wasn't going to rally and recover this time. I'm sure Lisa helped her cross over with a deep faith and dignity.

The next caller was Erica, who had a visitation from her sister. Erica is an empath. She feels other people's energies. She feels their feelings. Her sisters were twins, and one crossed over from a bicycle accident. The twins were on a bike together. They came around a corner and another bike was there, and they collided. One twin was injured and eventually healed, but the other suffered brain damage and never recovered. Erica was about eight years old, and her sister came to her. Her sister was at the end of her bed. Erica remembered me saying that was how I saw my first spirit. Like me, she knew nothing about the spirit world. "I woke up, and there she was at the end of my bed, smiling! She just smiled!" Erica described. She said her sister was iridescent. I told her that her sister smiling was a great sign! I asked about the living twin, and she said that they still always communicate! Twins are usually extremely connected no matter what dimension they live in—it's an amazing thing. I picked up on James, her father, who is with the twin sister in heaven. I told her that her dad is the protector for her sisters and for her. He said one day they will all be together again. She started to cry. It's always good to have happy tears knowing our loved ones are watching over us! I told Erica she was a truly pure, good soul and had others' best interests at heart. It's unfortunate that not all empaths are pure. Some want to control others.

The next caller, Elizabeth, was from canyon country in California. She felt spirits more than she saw them. She got tingling sensations, and she sometimes felt a touch on her shoulder or arm; she could sense that a spirit was there, though she did not always know which person it was, even though their energy was all around her. She said when her best friend died of cancer, Elizabeth was with her every step of the way. Her friend went to Germany for an alternative treatment, which did not work. About a week before she passed away, Elizabeth felt and sensed something terribly wrong. She saw something at the foot of her bed—a beam of light that then floated over her. She intuited that it was a group of angels or spirit guides. They told her everything would be okay, but her friend would cross over. They didn't speak aloud to her, but they communicated with thought. I told her that was a good sign. Most who have a euphoric near-death experience don't want to come back to Earth; they feel so peaceful on the other side. I told her I was happy that her friend went to a "good neighborhood." Elizabeth was blessed that she found comfort in this. "It's not your imagination; it's God's workers saying she's going to be taken care of and that you will see her again one day," I said. She was pretty sure that her friend came and visited her, because she got a familiar tingling down her arm. Then I picked up on the energy of her other friend who visited her as well. I felt the other girl who died made her stressed out. The husband didn't take care of her, and she had a stressful time through her illness and passing. One of the greatest gifts you can give to a friend or loved one is to make sure they feel love and have a peaceful crossing over.

Who do you think will be waiting for you when you cross over to the other side? I asked that question on my podcast recently. A nice lady named Louise called and was thrilled to talk about this topic. She repeated my intro when I said, "You know, none of us are getting out of here alive." Louise had lost her brother, as well as her adult son. She said I used the word *lost* often when I spoke, even though I knew spirits were with us. I was impressed with that insight and continue to reflect on why I use the words I do. Louise said there was a twenty-year interval between her son and her brother crossing over. I told her I couldn't imagine losing a son. Louise has done a lot of grief work. As Louise struggled to find peace, she said there was one thing that gave her comfort. She experienced the same thing when both her son and her brother passed. When we cross over, we are met with a special embodiment of love.

For Louise, it's always been light, white or pink, and the colors are translucent and vibrant. We are met with the light and the envelopment of love. She said that's what happens. Even if we are alone and not attached to anyone on the planet, we are met by that embodiment of love. I told her I always said that when we died, it wasn't how rich you were, how famous you were, or how good you looked. It was about your deeds. Were you compassionate? Were you kind to others? Did you love with all your heart? Did you live with a clear conscience? All that matters is love. God is love, and love is God. My father always said that. He wrote in my prayer book, "God is love, love is God, we love you.—Mother and Dad."

I asked Louise what made her think the light was white or

pink. She said she had been meditating since the '80s, either in a group or on her own. Before the passing of close loved ones, she would feel a deep centering feeling like a wholeness. The only word she could identify it with was *love*. And it was momentary. She also saw visions of "light shadows." When her loved ones passed, she experienced this. She said it was hard for her to explain the light, but it enveloped her like a shawl. Her son came to her moments after his passing, and that incredible force of light was there.

I told Louise that her story reminded me of people who had had near-death experiences. They said the colors they saw were indescribably vibrant. It was like nothing we experienced here. You couldn't explain what the color really was. It was like you became color. The sound of music was indescribable as well. It was like you felt it, as if you became its vibration. I began to pick up on her brother and her son. I received the name John, who was her brother, and the middle name Michael. I told her she had summoned her brother and her son to us. How beautiful! They showed me that a photo fell off the wall or off the counter. She said, "Yes, yes!" Her son told me he had pushed it down.

It always amazes me how spirits can use their energy to make things happen and move things! They make lights go on and off. They make sure you hear their favorite song. It reminded me of the movie *Ghost* with Demi Moore and Patrick Swayze—the scene where Swayze's character learned to make a penny slide down the wall. It makes me feel that spirits are becoming more knowledgeable on how to make themselves known.

I told her, "I feel that your son has learned this. He's showing me a birthday that just passed." She said, "We both just had birthdays that just passed." I said, "He knows you still celebrate his birthday."

Louise said she carried him for ten months. I said he didn't want to come to Earth. He took long naps. She said that she always thought that he was delaying his arrival. Her son showed me his shirt, and I asked if she sometimes wore his shirt. She said, "I used to, but I am saving it for his child." He knew she was going to give his things to his child.

I then asked her if she was planning to move. She said yes and that a man who specialized in lowballing wanted to buy her house. I did not have a good feeling about him, and I told her, "When it sounds too good to be true, it usually is." I told her to sell it the right way and that the real estate market was booming at that time. She said she was leaving a complicated relationship and that selling to this man would be an easy way out.

I said, "Don't let that be a factor in selling your home the right way. You would be accepting an offer just to get out. Be patient. That's how the trickster energies could bring more chaos into your life. When you are down, they try to take advantage. There's too much chaos around this. It doesn't feel right to me!"

She said, "Oh my God! I just saw my son's light! It's iridescent blue!"

I told her, "That's a sign that he agrees with the guidance I'm giving you! In fact, he's the one who gave me the information."

She said she got goose bumps.

"Well, goose bumps mean that we are speaking the truth!" I said. She had indeed received validation. "Don't be bullied by the relationship thing," I said, and I told her to put herself first and take the time and care to do what was best for her.

She said she felt so grounded talking to me about this.

It's always my honor when people allow me to help them. Again, you will hear me say this many times throughout this book, but we are most susceptible to trickster energies when we don't feel like ourselves. After a breakup, during a health or financial crisis, or because of some other stressor, there are definitely good friends who will come to us, but there are also predatory forces. I would caution anyone against doing a business deal or moving in quickly with someone during a period like this. We make the best decisions when we are feeling the best about ourselves, and I believe her son came through to help her feel the strength and confidence to start making better choices.

Next, an excited voice came on saying, "Oh my goodness, I can't believe I got through!" This was Meghan. She said she could cry right at that moment, because she had been following me for years. I told her it meant the world to me that she followed me. It's people like Meghan who allow me to do the work that I love to do, and I thanked her. Meghan was calling from New Jersey. I asked her who she thought would be waiting for her when she crossed over.

She said, "I know my dad and a couple of friends, but I think what happens is that we actually have a plan when we get to the other side, and we are supposed to help people here."

I told her, "I believe we are all interconnected, and I believe that we need to live with empathy and kindness. Not to a point where we hurt ourselves but to be kind, owning our own self-love. I feel, though, that we are interconnected, and this COVID pandemic proves that we all have a responsibility to protect each other. When we wear a mask, we show how we are protecting others and ourselves."

She said that putting compassion and love for humanity first was a message we all needed to learn, and if this was what we needed to experience to become more aware of this, to care for other people, then this was a deeply powerful message.

I asked Meghan if I could ask her something, and then I told her I saw the initial *B*.

She said, "Is it Bill? I had a friend who just passed named Bill, and my grandfather was also named Bill."

I told her I thought it was her friend Bill, and right at that moment, the light above me flickered. Meghan said he was strong. I asked if he was young, and she said, "Yes, he was only fifty-two years old." I told her that Bill was grateful to her. She said she loved him dearly.

I said, "He is telling me he was like a brother to you," and she said, "From the moment I met him, I felt he was like a brother." I told Meghan that Bill wanted her to know that his transition was good. I added, "He also said that when you pass over, he will be there for you. He said he won't be the first in line, but he will be there. He's saying something was confusing about his funeral."

At this point, Meghan explained that Bill's wife was also her good friend and that they'd had a falling-out. She went on to explain that the relationship between herself and Bill's wife was not healthy, so she hadn't seen them much, and that she'd felt a little guilty about losing touch with him. She started crying as she explained that her relationship with his wife was codependent and draining. As she spoke, I told her that Bill understood. I asked Meghan if apologies were exchanged at Bill's funeral, and while Meghan said no words were spoken, she did feel more closure at the funeral, spiritually. She went on to explain that Bill's wife was very needy, too dependent, and she'd felt she had to build a boundary. At this point, Bill started to come through again, and I told her I had the sense that Bill's wife had wronged him deeply. He told me that when Meghan was in their lives, it made his life much more manageable.

I said, "She was *not* easy! He said he had had enough of his wife, and when you were in the picture, his world was much more tolerable. All he wanted to do was put his earphones on and mute his wife out. He's saying his wife was so annoying."

She started laughing! "Yes, yes!" she said. "Definitely!"

I continued, "When you were around, he wanted to be near you. He said you were like a breath of fresh air to him," and she said, "Oh my, yes! He said that to me when I first met him! Verbatim, 'You are like a breath of fresh air to me!'"

I told Meghan that Bill was warning her not to go back to her old habits with his wife, that she was too draining and Meghan was too nice. I advised Meghan, "Don't do that out of guilt! She's just too draining for you! She's just too exhausting. You know what she needs?" I asked. "She needs a good therapist! That's what she needs!"

I asked Meghan if anyone ever suggested therapy to Bill's wife. She said, "I was debating, but it wouldn't have been well received."

I said, "No wonder he died at fifty-two. He couldn't handle it all!" I laughed and added, "I hope she's not listening to this show." She said no, she wouldn't be. I was relieved.

When spirits come through, I don't have a filter. My friends would say this is true of me in regular life (sorry!), but it's definitely true when I'm reading. I just say what I am hearing in real time. This is one of the many reasons why people can become so emotional when I read, because they are hearing the words not as I would say them but as I am hearing them. I want to point that out before I continue this story, because I've spent quite a bit of time talking about being positive and not wishing ill on people. I certainly mean no offense to Bill's wife (although I'm not looking forward to being trapped in an elevator with her). I just want to take a moment to explain that it is not my place to judge. I am here to communicate and to translate what I am hearing the best way I can.

I asked Meghan if Bill had been ill and if he had cancer, and she said yes. I will take a moment here to express my view that when we are ill and we aren't happy, things can fester inside of us, and that stress causes health problems. Again, this is why I encourage everyone to be mindful of the energies around them and take time for self-care. This is another area where I am continuously impressed and grateful for younger generations, who have done such a great job in destigmatizing self-care.

I told Meghan that she felt Bill's stress contributed to his health problems. She said, "Yes! I knew it! I felt it!" I said to Meghan that Bill used his illness as a get-out-of-jail-free card. He was too nice to leave his wife and loved her in his own way, but he didn't want to be around anymore. He was done. I explained again that Bill was telling me to tell her not to get stuck in that rut again, and she thanked me. I told Meghan she had a huge heart and wanted to save the world, but that it wouldn't be good for her to get stuck in that again. I explained to her that Bill was definitely there and he was grateful to her. I told her I was sure that her grandfather Bill was there, too, but the one who had more to say tonight was her friend, who was trying to keep her out of harm's way. She said that she needed this more than anything!

I wanted to share this story again for three reasons you will hear me say over and over again: 1) be mindful of the energy you have around you, 2) be careful of the stress you internalize, as it can impact your health, and 3) I'm sorry if I offend you when I am reading—I'm just doing as I'm told!

The next caller was originally from California but had since moved to Idaho. I asked if I knew her, and she said we'd known each other a long time ago. Her name was Sandy. She said we'd studied with the same teacher. I told her how I believed that the teacher had really changed and gone from being a positive energy to a demonic energy. That happens to people who connect with the other side and are not protecting themselves. Sandy said she felt many energies and worked with hospice care for years. This is amazing work, and my thanks go out to anyone who performs this incredible service. Sandy said she was able to help her kids and their friends by teaching them that there was another side to life. She used this knowledge to help guide her children to stop behaviors that were destructive to themselves.

We are measured not by the money we make or the fame we achieve but by the love and kindness and goodness of our actions. Sandy agreed with me that positive attracted positive. I said to Sandy that she must have had stories to share as a result of her work with hospice patients. Sandy said she spent a great deal of time helping her patients prepare for the other side, and just being there with them was incredibly special. She said when she got ready in the morning, she saw a flickering blue light. Sandy said she had spirits that came to her. She felt them. She said she asked them, "Why are you coming to me? What are you trying to tell me?" Then she said she concentrated on the spirits and tried to bring the white light around her. She explained that her brother-in-law came to ask her to help his nephew. She asked me why I thought spirits were coming to her. I explained to Sandy that spirits were probably coming to her because no one else would listen!

We as a people live with a tremendous amount of emotion and fear. Sandy said she was able to help people with their transition to the other side. Recently, she said, a family friend had been coming to her. She said this friend looked at things with rose-colored glasses and didn't like to see anything bad. Sandy said she thought differently and not everything was wonderful. I told Sandy that she and I belonged to the same club.

"This is amazing," Sandy said and shared that she had always had an ability to feel the Earth's movement. She said she didn't know where it came from.

"Oh my God!" I said. "What do you think about earthquakes? Is that why you got out of California?" I asked her.

She said, "Yes!"

I told Sandy I kept feeling earthquake energy. She said she thought it was going to happen along the coast and it would happen within the next couple of months. (This was in January 2021.) Sandy said that before the Northridge earthquake, she was up all night pacing the ground. She said she could feel it, and she went to bed ten minutes before it happened. I said people had to take their paintings off the wall and artifacts from above their beds. Mirrors, too, needed to come down. She said it was important to have an earthquake kit and water and other things available in case the earth did start shaking. She told her kids to have a pair of shoes by the bed, as well as some clothes and a flashlight. I said that because of COVID, people were stocking up anyway and that maybe it was a blessing in disguise. She said people forgot to stay safe and to have things available if there was an earthquake. (So here's a side note. I'm wondering if there will be an earthquake before this book is published or soon after!)

I asked, "How does the Earth talk to you?"

She said, "It's weird, Char. I will get physical symptoms. Like a headache, or I may get a rash." I explained that when my sister had an issue with the trigeminal nerve, her doctor told her to go outside barefoot on the grass and ground herself. It helped her. Sandy is a water person and loves the water; that is what grounds her. She gets amazing messages in the water or in the shower. What Sandy described happens to many of us.

I asked if the hospice patients saw spirits waiting for them at the foot of the bed. So many people would reach up and smile before they would transition. There is one very special person she told us about.

Here is Sandy's story about Martha:

I was with Martha and her husband for several months. When Martha was at the end of her life, she had rapid breathing, which many people have before they cross over. Her family came, and her husband was there. She took her last breath. She reached up with her hands. The family said their goodbyes, and I called her doctor for the time of death. Then all of a sudden, Martha started moving, and her family was incredibly confused and asked what was going on. I explained to them that sometimes people will do that. Their muscles move involuntarily. It's not unusual, and it happens. But then Martha woke up! I don't remember exactly what happened, but she woke up! She was as clear as day. She knew everybody by name, and she looked at me and in an excited voice said, "Jesus does *not* look like the pictures we portray of him!" She said it clear as day. And then she said, "Why am I back here?" And I said I didn't know. Martha said, "I don't want to be back here. I saw my mom and my daddy," and then she went on and on about all the people she saw. I told her there was a reason she was back here. And she lived exactly a year from that day. I asked what Jesus looked like. Martha told me Jesus's skin was darker, much darker than how it was usually pictured. He didn't wear those robes we put on him, and his clothes were more like burlap. She was extremely disappointed in the pictures she had seen of him all her life.

After Sandy finished her story, I said, "Wow, this is a big lesson for all those people who are racist!" Sandy gave that a big amen, and we both laughed. To be clear, racism is a terrible plague in this country and around the world, and our laughter was a way of dealing with our shared horror. There is no place for racism in this world, and we all need to work harder and look within ourselves to do much, much better.

As Sandy continued to talk about how so many people would reach up and smile before they crossed over, I asked her about her own health. Sandy said her health was not good, and I told her that I was worried. I said I wanted to make sure that she was doing what the doctors were telling her to do. She said she had cancer and was on chemotherapy and radiation and taking the medicine she had been prescribed. She'd had several operations. She said she had just had a scan, and the results were coming the following week. I asked about her attitude and asked if she was imagining the battleships in her body destroying the bad cells. She said, "Yes, I sure do, and part of my calling is to reach out to other people who have cancer and try to help others even though I'm going through this as well." She explained that she got a great deal of positive energy knowing that she could still help others even though she was going through it herself. She said they gave her a fifty-fifty chance and had twice given her four to six months to live. I told her that she was a miracle because she was an angel on Earth.

Sandy said she felt her job wasn't done here yet and that there were more people she needed to help! I agreed. She said a woman came to her support group who just had a mammogram result showing an area of concern. Sandy offered to accompany her the following day for her ultrasound. She told her, "I will go with you and hold your hand, and we will go through this together."

I told Sandy I was honored that she had called in to the show. She is among the many unsung heroes to whom we are all grateful for doing what they do. I thanked Sandy for teaching us and asked everyone listening to send healing energy to her along with me. I told Sandy she was a teacher for all of us and a teacher for me. She asked if anyone was with her, and I said I saw an A or M. She said yes to that, and I got the name *Margaret*. I knew it was both her mom and her grandma. They said they would be there to meet her when she crossed over. I felt like I made a new friend and was honored to learn as much as I did from Sandy.

We live in a physical world, and we live in an energetic world. Whether you know it or not, we are all influenced by energy. Einstein's theory of relativity explains that $E=MC^2$. Energy does not stay stagnant. It has to go somewhere. Or, as those of us who are not theoretical physicists like to say, "What goes around comes around." Energy is enhanced at different times. Everyone's astrological chart points out when the energy is better for them to sign contracts or pursue the energy of love, to sell or buy a home, or to pay more attention to health issues. Many people feel an energy shift when there is a full moon. It is a known fact that hospitals have more emergencies during a full moon.

Psychic Main Points

∗ Letting go is natural and part of the process of life.
∗ As psychic intuitives, we can see letting go as a way of completing cycles and creating new beginnings.
∗ The more connected you are intuitively, the more you can help yourself and others in the letting-go process.
∗ We all have an expiration date.
∗ When it's time for our loved ones to move on, we need to be unselfish and allow them to ascend to heaven.

Psychic Journal Practice

Get your I AM PSYCHIC Journal.
Answer these questions:

∗ After reading this chapter, how do you view letting go?
∗ Is there anything (or anyone) that you need to let go of? (List them in your journal.)
∗ Are there any people you need to release and forgive?
∗ Have you left instructions for your loved ones? Is your house in order?
∗ If you were to let go, forgive, release, how would your life change?

Use the Char Tip in this chapter as a process to let go of everything and everyone that you need to.

When we know it's time for our loved ones to move on, it is our responsibility to be unselfish and give them permission to go. Our love and need for them could keep them here even though their physical bodies are worn out.

4

SPIRITS AND VISITATIONS

~~~~~~

What you will learn in this chapter: When you mention words like psychic or intuition or even topics like communicating with those who have died, one of the first things people will think about is "ghosts"! Thanks to movies and television, there are a lot of misconceptions about spirits who have passed over to the other side. This chapter is less interactive, but filled with important information about what happens when we die and why it is important.

~~~~~~

When I tell people I'm a psychic, they often ask me about things like haunted houses and other things they have seen on television and in the movies. As I've said several times throughout this book, there are positive and negative energies all around us (see, I told you I was going to remind you of this!). When most people think about a home being "haunted," they go straight to the negative and all of the bone-chilling imagery that comes with whichever Hollywood horror movie gives you the most nightmares. (For me, that would be just about all of them! For a person whom some might describe as a witch, I'm a true scaredy-cat! I'll take Disney over Dracula any day!)

Positive Spirits

Bad spirits seem to get all the attention! But before we get into the negative spirits in houses, I want to spend a minute to talk about the wonderful energies that we can discover in a home or bring to a new home. In an earlier chapter, I already shared how my toddler great-nephew guided his parents to a home they loved. But I also know many, many stories of how people felt that their home chose them. How does a home choose you? Well, you might feel a warm feeling as you walk in the door, or a bird might appear on a branch outside the window as you tour the kitchen, or a favorite song might play as you pull up to the open house. Whatever it is, however nontraditional your logic in making such a big decision may seem, I would advise that you trust your intuition. If something feels right (and let me stress that feeling right intuitively is very, very different from finding something that is supposedly "too good to be true"), it may be that you are being led to the right path by your spirit guides.

Real estate agents often refer to a house as having "good bones," and what I like about that description is that it acknowledges a history and literally the foundation of what makes a home a home. If a home is built with love and enjoyed fully, there may be some spirit guides who will visit the home from time to time to spread their protective energies.

Spirits who may be unsettled and not have had a positive experience crossing over may look for vehicles to use their trickster energies, and a home is certainly a place where trickster energies can linger. On one of my shows, I had a caller who said she had lived in a house for more than nine years. She said that right after she moved in, she knew that she wasn't there alone. It wasn't just her and a couple of cats. She wondered if I could pick up on anything or anyone there. She said she didn't feel threatened but she had gotten "creeped out" a couple of times, because some things that happened just didn't make sense and that she mostly felt the energy of a woman.

Shortly after she and her husband moved in, their relationship deteriorated. She said the activities had seemed to increase in recent years, and that when she was going through a painful experience, the incidents in the house seemed to increase. She spoke about a dark shadow flitting about the house and feeling a tingling on one side of her body like an electric shock. I suggested that she get sage and cleanse the house. I explained **that just because someone knocked on your door, it didn't mean you had to let them in.**

I told her that I didn't think the energy in the house was causing the problems in her marriage. I explained to her that it was my sense that there was a problem in the communication between the two of them and it was time to break up. That said, trickster energies do like to feed on that kind of chaotic energy. I told her to go to a natural foods or metaphysical or crystal store and purchase some bundles of sage. I then shared with her, as I do again here, one of the prayers of protection I say every time before I do a reading:

Anything that is in, near, around, or about me that is not of light, go back to where you came from and turn to light if you choose—but stay away from me!

I advised her to burn the sage around all the doors and the windows and demand the negative energy to go away. You can also burn palo santo. I said to her, and I say to everyone who asks me about negative energies, **no one and nothing has**

power over you unless you give it to them. Not a living person or a spirit. You are in control of your own free will.

I asked her if her cats felt the energy. She said, "Oh gosh! I had one who jumped and her ears went down." I explained to her that it sounded like a trickster energy to me and told her to please use the sage and use the prayer of protection. I shared my view that if the cat was scared, that was worrisome. Everybody who knows animals knows how sensitive they are to energies, so I again urge you—if you won't listen to your own intuition, listen to your cats, dogs, horses, birds. What are they telling you? You want and deserve peaceful energy in your home. You have the power to change it.

CHAR TIP:
CLEANSING YOUR HOUSE

The Native Americans use sage to cleanse their spaces. You can get white sage most anywhere, including Whole Foods. Light the sage and put a ceramic bowl or shell under it so you don't start a fire. It will catch the embers. Start at the front door and go around the entire home, including the corners. I went traveling through the Cotswolds in England. There was a little village we came to. The first house was round and had no corners. The last house driving through the village was round as well. They built them round "so the devil couldn't hide in the corners."

Burn incense, such as lavender, myrrh, sandalwood, and dragon's blood.

You can invite good spirits by using protection oils, such as Holy Spirit, uncrossing, and fiery wall of protection. You can also carve your name on a white, red, or purple candle and put the protection oils and lavender oil on it, and ask your guardian angels and spirit guides to protect you. Make sure you let the candle burn to the bottom.

If a spirit is not welcome in your home, demand them to go away and tell them that they are not welcome there. Invite them to the white light, but demand that they go away!

Burn palo santo like the Inca and their descendants do.

Another way to cleanse your home is to put salt in every corner of the house.

Using the rosary helps many people.

You can wear a hamsa or an evil eye to ward off any negativity.

Frankincense and myrrh oils are used for protection of health.

Jeanine's and Seth's Stories

Sometimes the connections I make, like the stories I tell, take time to make sense. I had a caller on my show, Jeanine from Salt Lake, who had been following me for years. Jeanine is intuitive and, like many other mothers, is particularly attuned to her children. Jeanine says she knows things before they happen, and like many, she says she becomes more intuitive around the full moon—like getting a charge from an electric socket. I asked if her kids thought she was a witch, and she said no, but they knew they couldn't lie to her because she would always catch them. I told Jeanine I saw her being a grandma. (She has two grandkids now, and I saw another eventually on the way.) Then I asked Jeanine if she ever went to a graveyard. She said she often did and felt very connected to a lot of the people there. I warned Jeanine to protect herself and use the white light of protection and mirrored egg, because while she enjoyed walking around the graveyard, she didn't really know what energies she was connecting to, and she needed to be more careful. Jeanine said she liked going to the cemetery to see her sister and her brother and found comfort in her walks. She also said her son's best friend had passed away, and she wanted me to pick up on it. I asked Jeanine to have her son call back and arrange a reading with me, but due to some production issues she missed my invitation.

All week, I thought about Jeanine's son and was hoping he would call me, but I didn't hear anything. The following week, I asked my listeners to call in with their stories experiencing a miracle. After a few other callers, we received a call from a Salt Lake number and I hoped it might be Jeanine, but it was a young man. After I thanked him for calling and said how nice it was to have a male caller, he informed me that he was calling in at the request of his mother. I immediately asked him if he was the young man who had lost a close friend.

After he said yes, I told him I had been thinking about him all week. His name was Seth. Before I did the reading, as always, I started out with my protection prayer. I picked up on Seth's grandfather Richard. Then I got the name John, Seth's father and Richard's son, who was living. I said that Seth's friend's death was not an intentional suicide and that he had overdosed accidentally. Then I got a C initial, which was his friend's first initial. I got the name *Cal*, but his name was Caelen, which was close enough for me. I picked up on Caelen's mom's last name initial. He was showing me that Seth had something of his. Seth said he had Caelen's backpack. Caelen was telling me that Seth tried really hard to get him off drugs. I knew that one of the reasons Seth was suffering is that he felt like he'd failed his friend. Seth confirmed my narrative. Caelen started apologizing for messing up. He talked about how they would hang out until two or three in the morning. I knew that the two of them were close and that Caelen was a deep thinker with a strong, creative mind. I saw music or writing.

Caelen knew that Seth had done his best to try to save him. I saw that a girl had disappointed Caelen. He was planning on breaking up with her. I felt he was chemically imbalanced and self-medicated. Caelen thanked Seth for trying to help his mom. He definitely had healing gifts. I told Seth that it seemed like he had worked hard to save Caelen and to know that he hadn't failed, that he had done his best, and that Caelen's death was not his fault and he should not take responsibility. I asked Seth if that made sense to him, and he said yes. I also explained that it was my feeling that Caelen was getting help on the other side and that Seth should continue to pray for him.

Then I saw Seth taking a new business opportunity with his former manager. I asked Seth if he had been finding feathers. He said yes.

I said, "That is Caelen."

He said, "I remember telling him out loud, 'If you are ever near me, drop a feather or a dime.'"

I said, "That's your friend."

Seth said he had found a couple of feathers and put them up on his truck's visor. I explained that it took a great deal of energy to get those feathers to him and that said to me that Caelen was in a good place and starting to get the healing he needed. I kept repeating that Caelen didn't want Seth to feel bad, because he didn't want Seth to carry that weight and that he wanted Seth to know when he received those feathers, it was a gift from him! He thanked me and hung up the phone. After we hung up, I thanked my producer, Tony, for putting that call through, and he said he didn't even know who was on the phone, that the lines were full. To me, that's another example of intuition kicking in—in this case, for Tony. After the show, I received a Facebook message from Seth's mom, Jeanine, that she had been the other Salt Lake caller that we'd lost. It was further confirmation that our call with Seth was meant to be.

I also want to take a moment to reflect on this story, which unfortunately is not unique. Far too many of us have lost people to addiction, and over the years, I have spoken to hundreds of people who blame themselves for not doing more to prevent someone's death. I would like to share in my experience with the spirit world that not once has a spirit energy contacted me to cast blame. Always, always, it is to thank the person, to try to unburden them from any feelings of guilt, and to show love. I would also encourage anyone who is struggling to help someone with an addiction or needs help themselves not to suffer in silence. I have a client who is an alcoholic. She and her husband like to drink every night. Their teenage son started to take drugs. Unfortunately, he has a heart condition. Drugs could be deadly for him. I told the mother that it was hypocritical for her to insist he stop taking drugs, because of her alcohol problem. I'm happy to say she has stopped drinking. There is no shame in asking for help, quite the opposite. Asking for help is a blessing. Find a drug rehab in your area or go to Al-Anon or Alcoholics Anonymous for help. There are many drug abuse centers that you can find.

Psychic Main Points

* Spirits and visitations are not usually like what you see in movies and television.
* Good movies to watch are *Ghost, Field of Dreams, The Ghost and Mrs. Muir, The Five People You Meet in Heaven, The Lovely Bones, It's a Wonderful Life, Poltergeist, Heaven Is for Real, Heaven Can Wait, Defending Your Life,* and *Oh, God!*
* Yes, there are negative spirits, but there are also positive spirits as well.
* We can communicate with spirits.
* Use the prayer of protection and sage to rid yourself of negative spirits and energies.
* Own your power and your intuitive ability!
* Look for a good therapist or support group that works with grief and losing a loved one.

Psychic Journal Practice

Get your I AM PSYCHIC Journal.
Answer these questions:

* Have you had any experiences of spirits—positive or negative?
* If you could communicate with any loved one who has passed over to the other side, who would it be? Why? (You can list more than one.)

In your journal, write this loved one a letter, expressing your love for them and your desire to have safe, positive communication with them. You can ask them to give you a clear sign that they are there. Watch closely to see if you get an answer.

For all answers, let your mind go blank, and trust the first image or thought that comes to you. Let go, and focus on letting the answer come through. Get out of the way, and allow the wisdom to come through. You may feel goose bumps as validation. You just may have an all-knowing feeling that your thought is a truthful answer.

5

MIRACLES

~~~~~~

What you will learn in this chapter: Like the previous chapter, this chapter is less interactive than most, but filled with stories that will show you how miracles occur. You will also learn briefly about near-death experiences and why they are important.

Write in your journal a miracle that you have experienced.

Share a story about a near-death experience, either yours or someone else's.

~~~~~~

Laurie's Story

Another caller on the miracle show was Laurie. Laurie was on her way to her spiritualist church. Laurie described how she lived on a mountain road in British Columbia with a steep cliff on one side. As she was driving with a friend, she hit a patch of black ice and lost control of the vehicle. At that moment, the most peaceful feeling came over her. She said she'd never felt anything like it before, a feeling of utter peace and calm. Meanwhile, her friend was absolutely terrified and screaming. Laurie began calming down her friend, saying, "I've got this," as they headed off the cliff. As they were driving off the mountain, hitting trees, her friend screaming, she said, "It's okay, Di. We're going over. We're going nose-first." Laurie said that no sooner did she say the words than her vehicle, a Toyota 4Runner, turned right around and, instead of going nose-first, turned around and went backward. She watched as an enormous tree carved her door into a V. Laurie was not wearing a seat belt. (Please, always wear a seat belt!) Laurie described flipping around in that vehicle, until she landed—*boom*! She then asked her friend if she was all right, and she answered, "I think so, but you're on top of me!" The SUV was on its side, and they crawled out of the back. The engine was screaming. Laurie saw her friend sitting on a log. She asked her if she was okay. Her friend said her finger was bleeding. Laurie told her she had a mini pad in her purse, but then realized she couldn't see. She crawled back to her car and turned off the engine, which was racing, and then she saw, as if someone had placed them there, her glasses folded up right next to her! Laurie didn't have a scratch! Nothing! She told me she had all the pictures to prove it! All of a sudden, they noticed people at the top of the mountain looking down at them, yelling to ask if they were all right. She recognized a friend of hers and called to him to call her husband. She said they had landed in a low spot, but it was still fifty feet down from where they went off the road. Laurie thanked God and her angels for protecting her and her friend.

Elizabeth's Story

A listener named Elizabeth called. She explained how, back in 2008, her brother was in liver failure and needed a transplant. Elizabeth went through all the testing to be a donor, but as she had ulcerative colitis, she was rejected as a potential donor. Elizabeth's partner spoke up and said, "Let me donate." That in itself was a miracle, and she and Elizabeth flew from California to Wisconsin, where Elizabeth's brother lived, to do all the testing. It turned out that Elizabeth's partner was actually a closer match to her brother than Elizabeth was! The transplant was an eighteen-hour surgery, and afterward, both moved to the ICU. The next morning, Elizabeth's brother was failing badly. He had developed a clot in the artery supplying the new liver, and there was no blood flow to the liver all night long. The doctors sat Elizabeth and her family down and said his chance of surviving was less than 1 percent. They moved him to the top of the list and told them they needed to find another donor within the next twenty-four hours—impossible. Even though Elizabeth's brother was just hanging on, they brought him back to surgery, removed his liver, and treated him for his clot—a procedure that had not previously been performed in the United States. The doctors were hoping her partner's liver would remain viable after not having blood flow for more than twelve hours. They put her partner's liver back into her brother, and the next morning, he had blood flow. Elizabeth said it had been almost thirteen years since the transplant and her brother was doing fantastically! Elizabeth said despite the doctor's prognosis, she had known her brother would survive. For Elizabeth's brother, there were three miracles—that Elizabeth's partner was a match (the doctors said that was one in a million!), that they were able to do the transplant in time, and that after the clot, her brother recovered with no damage to his new liver. I find in life things come in threes, and it is incredible that they had three miracles in one! I also believe that Elizabeth's partner being a closer-than-a-sibling match to her brother teaches us a great spiritual lesson about family and love. What a pure example of two of my favorite sayings: "It was meant to be" and "There is nothing more powerful than love."

Sandy's Story

Sandy called in from Toronto, Canada. She called in about two miracles she had while driving—both were close calls with trucks. In both instances, Sandy doesn't know how she survived and believes she went into a state of shock until she was safely out of danger. It was as if her angels took over the steering wheel.

Sandy's stories jogged my memory about a time when I was in Michigan driving on a two-lane highway called Middlebelt with my mother. We were climbing up a steep hill at about forty-five miles per hour. All of a sudden in front of me was a huge semitruck coming downhill right at us! I swerved to the right and drove onto the shoulder to avoid the truck. Miraculously, there was a solid gravel lane at the side of the road (oftentimes, the road is bordered by ditches or other structures that would make driving on it impossible or deadly), and we avoided a head-on collision. The mistake occurred because there was roadwork and the person directing traffic accidentally signaled for the truck to proceed. **Mistakes happen, and so do miracles!**

All three of us had angels preventing something far worse from happening.

My sister Alicia experienced a miracle while driving:

> Back when I was a student at the University of Michigan, I was driving home from class in Ann Arbor to my home in West Bloomfield. Between the darkness of the night and the heavy snowstorm, visibility was poor, and I veered off at the wrong turn at the fork in the expressway. Foolishly, I tried to quickly turn the car back onto the expressway, and my car started to spin out of control in the snow. My prayers must have been heard, because when the car finally stopped spinning, it was headed in the right direction and on the correct road. That was truly a miracle, but it was also a lesson. **I have learned that sometimes wrong turns happen for a reason.** I was young, exhausted from a long day of classes, and probably shouldn't have been driving late, in the dark during a blizzard. But what I really shouldn't have done was try to dangerously reenter the expressway—of course my car skidded. It's worth spending the extra five minutes to take the wrong exit and then get back on safely. It could be that you are being protected. Have you ever accidentally taken a wrong exit only to come back onto the highway and discover you just missed an accident? Taken a wrong turn and found a stray dog? Or maybe you just discovered a Starbucks when you wanted a coffee? Whatever it is, my advice is go with the wrong turn, trust your intuition, and try to recognize the wonder of the unexpected whenever you can.

CHAR TIP:
TESTIMONIAL

On the subject of car accidents, I want to include a testimonial from a client, Wanda Baugher:

I watched Char on a DIRECTV special. She really impressed me, so I obtained a reading.

First off, she told me all my kids' names. She said, "One keeps telling me she *is* going to college." (We didn't think she would, by the way her life was headed. But she did and became a registered nurse and is currently thinking about furthering her education.)

Also, Char told me my youngest, in third grade at the time, was having a hard time in school and that she had two specific disabilities. A few months later, the school wanted to test her, and she did have two different learning disabilities. Char told me one child would hold a job title and the other would have a creative gift.

The child with learning disabilities could sing and learned to play the guitar at age fourteen and won a few singing contests. She tried out for *American Idol* at age eighteen and was asked to reaudition. I was going to take her for a second round to reaudition, but she told me she felt bad and didn't want to go stand in line again. A few months later, she was hospitalized with multiple sclerosis. She lost her ability to play the guitar for over a year. She never tried to sing professionally or in local contests again.

At the time of my reading, my nephew had just lost his infant girl in a car wreck. Char knew my nephew's name and his daughter's name. What really got to my heart was that Char said his five-month-old baby kept saying it was not her daddy's fault.

Char did not know this, but my nephew's wife and her family kept calling my nephew a murderer, blaming him for their child's death. My nephew was driving, but it was his wife who put the car seat in the car and their baby in the car seat. The car seat was put in wrong, and the baby was also not properly secured. The baby was thrown through the car window, and my nephew had to walk in a field to find his daughter. But the confirmation of the baby telling Char that her death was not her daddy's fault was so wonderful to hear.

I asked about my job, and she told me I would hold a title job. Which most of my jobs were titled positions. Current job title is Field Interviewer. I just ask questions. I don't have to write anything, so forgive me of any writing errors in this email.

Char told me it was my choice to remarry my husband, which I did after sixteen years! Took that long to feel secure enough to remarry.

I wished I could have gotten on the air tonight to tell everyone all of this. You were the first person to ever give me names and situations. Then watch as events unfolded for twenty years.

~~~~~~~~~~~~~~~~~~~

I bring up this testimonial because unfortunately, car accidents happen. People blame themselves, and they blame others. You've heard me talk about fear of death, and one of the behaviors that comes with fear of death is blame and guilt. This is not to say that there are not accidents where there is a person, a road condition, or some other thing that clearly is at fault or causes the accident. But even in those terrible situations, they are still accidents. I did pick up on the improper car seat installation, but it was certainly not because their infant daughter wanted to blame her mother or father or for them to feel responsible. I believe it was her attempt to bring her parents peace. The father was driving, the mother improperly installed the car seat, both were responsible, but neither is to blame. When a child dies young, I believe we need to start with: What lessons did that child teach us? What can we learn from that child about love, forgiveness, and acceptance? If we can let go of our fear of death, we can let go of so much of the guilt and blame and hurt that comes with that fear and instead focus on the spirit and love that unites us all.

Psychic Main Points

* Do you tell your loved ones that you love them?
* If a loved one passed over unexpectedly, would you have guilt or unfinished business?
* Have you been in a relationship, broken up, and gotten back together? Sometimes people go back together for the wrong reasons, especially in dysfunctional relationships. But sometimes the two souls have to finish their karma, instead of being reincarnated again to complete it.
* Have you ever gotten lost but ended up somewhere you had wanted to find? Or have you been looking for something and while looking you find something else you had been trying to find for weeks? Sometimes our guides take us on a journey to help us find lost objects.
* When unfortunate circumstances happen and you are involved but they are not your fault, can you let go of that? Can you forgive yourself and others?

Psychic Journal Practice

Get your I AM PSYCHIC Journal.
  Do the following exercises:

* Has life ever put you in a position that caused a tragic or awkward circumstance for yourself or others that you had no control over? (Write how you coped with this and what you learned.)
* If someone else unintentionally caused these circumstances, were you able to forgive them? (Forgiveness is so important. We don't want to carry that anger within us.)
* Make a list of times you were divinely guided and protected.

6

DREAMS, FEELINGS, AND PREMONITIONS

What you will learn in this chapter: It's time to fine-tune your awareness of, and experience of, the ways that life reaches out to show you information about yourself and those you love. Here are some more stories of those who followed the signs and those who did not. Use them as examples for your own experiences.

Have you ever had a premonition that came to pass about something important? We asked some of the listeners on *Char-Vision*. Here are some of their responses.

Tony Sweet, the owner of UBNGo, was my engineer that evening, like all Fridays. Tony told us about a dream he had when he was a boy; he described it as more of a "feeling" than a dream. The feeling he had was a persistent unease about his uncle's dog, Dandy, whom Tony absolutely loved. Tony said he and Dandy were like best friends. They would always hang out together. That summer, when Tony was on vacation with his parents, his anxiety about Dandy hit an absolute peak; he kept having dreams about people wanting to kill Dandy, chasing him and trying to hurt him. When his father called home to check in with his uncle, Tony insisted his father ask his uncle about Dandy. His father said okay and said to his brother, "Tony wants to know about Dandy." His uncle answered that he'd had to put Dandy down. As in Tony's description, the blur between dreams and "a feeling" is something that many callers describe, and that soft space between conscious and unconscious thought can be hard to decipher. *Is this anxiety? Am I overthinking it?* When we are in a situation where we can't clearly define our thoughts, there is a tendency to be dismissive or to think our "feelings" are irrational because they can't be logically explained. My guidance to you, always, is to first ask yourself, *Is this my intuition telling me something? Is there a certainty in this "feeling" that is coming from a place of trust, a part of me that I know I should listen to and honor?*

I'm fortunate in that from a young age my parents honored the power of my intuition. When I was in my early twenties, we had a home in northern Michigan. One year, on the Fourth of July weekend, my parents were coming to visit my husband and me. I told my mother, "Tell Daddy to stay in the right lane." It is always bumper-to-bumper traffic going up north on the holiday weekend, and it's about a four-and-a-half-hour drive. The temptation to weave in and out of lanes to gain a few minutes here and there is overwhelming, but my mother was insistent that my father stay in the right lane. My parents always listened to my intuition since, as a child, I had proven that I "knew things" that couldn't be rationally explained. On that trip, my father fell asleep at the wheel. He swerved to the right and ended up on the shoulder. Had they been in any other lane, there would have been a terrible accident.

We had a caller from Michigan. She said she kept having a

dream over and over again of walking out of a building of some sort. She said that as she walked out of the building, she saw picnic tables and a huge hill and a lake and a big white house. Years later, she was sent to a summer camp in northern Michigan, and when she first saw the property, it was exactly what she had been dreaming of for years. She said she literally lost her breath. It took her a second because she had been having that dream for more than five years and it absolutely had come to life! She was thirteen years old, and it was the strongest premonition she had ever had. Twenty years later, she still thinks about it all the time. She's working at meditating and trying to connect with her intuition more.

Oftentimes, people tell me that the strongest premonitions they had were when they were young. This doesn't surprise me, because when we are younger, we have not yet learned to be so dismissive of our "feelings." It is only as we age that we become less trusting of our intuition, because so often, it can't be explained by logic or "rational" thinking. I am here to tell you that your intuition is rational. In many ways, your intuition may be the most rational thought you have—what thought could be more intelligent than one that comes from your deepest sense? When we think of intuitive skill or natural ability, we describe it as a gift—whether it is athletic, musical, mathematical, mechanical, literary. There are too many to name, but when we meet people with these "gifts," to us, it seems otherworldly, and we might even describe them as "God-given talents." While each of us have our own unique gifts from God, there are some gifts we all share, and one of them is our intuition. If there is one point I want to get across in this book, it is that **your intuition is a precious gift. Use it, listen to it, nurture it, and the more you do, the easier it will be for you to let go of your fears and fully live in this world.**

I've spoken to many people who have told me that premonitions in their dreams have come to pass. Sometimes these premonitions can be confusing, especially for children. One night, Mary Helen called in from South Carolina. She has had several premonitions. They always come in dreams. She shared that one of her first premonitions happened when she was about four years old, and that in it she saw her father pull a knife on her mother. When she woke up, she was distraught and thought, *Oh no! I don't want that to happen!* Shortly after her dream, there was a violent incident in which her father tried to stab her mother. Fortunately, her mother was safe and her parents got divorced, but for the longest time, Mary Helen felt deeply guilty. She was just a child, but she kept thinking, *Did I make this happen because I dreamed it?* She was confused, guilty, and upset. It took her a long time to realize it wasn't her fault—her dream hadn't caused anything. I told Mary Helen that this was an interesting comment, because her intuition didn't feel like a positive thing to own; instead, her intuition made her feel guilty or responsible because she saw a horrible event ahead of time.

This guilt is not uncommon. Often, people feel guilty because they *thought* it; they think they made it happen! But they didn't! It was a warning. It was a premonition. But if you don't understand your intuition or how accurate it can be, it can cause deep psychological trauma. Mary Helen said that at the time, because she was only four years old, nobody ever talked about what happened.

She then shared a story with us about her seventeen-year-old daughter. Earlier in the school year, Mary Helen's daughter had woken up distraught about a dream that felt like a premonition. She told her mother she'd had a dream that she was at school and she felt extremely lethargic and dizzy and she couldn't climb a set of stairs; she described the stairwell with many windows and told her mother she knew exactly what stairwell it was at the school. Mary Helen trusted her daughter's premonition immediately and told her to stay clear of that stairwell and not to accept food or drinks from anyone, including her friends. She said, "Maybe someone at school will try to slip something in your food or drink." Mary Helen was anxious when she sent her daughter to school, particularly because that was the first time her daughter had told her something like that and it came to her as soon as she woke up. Later that same day, some students had taken drugs in the bathroom, and they had to shut down the stairwell from her daughter's dream, because one of the kids who had taken drugs had passed out there! The dream was more about that feeling of being drugged and disoriented—she didn't take anything, but it happened to someone else in that school that very same day. Mary Helen recognizes that she and her daughter share the gift, and they have open conversations about it all the time. It warmed my heart because Mary Helen has also taught her daughter about the white light and the mirrored egg, which she has heard me talk about many times.

~~~~~~~~~~~~~~~~

CHAR TIP:
THE MIRRORED EGG

I want to make something clear. I learned about the mirrored egg from my friend Patti Negri. Patti is extremely good at getting rid of negative energies around people. We live in a physical world, and we live in an energetic world all at the same time. The world runs like a battery. There is always a positive and negative charge. We are all protected, but it is like Swiss cheese around us; there are little holes that trickster energies try to get in. I make it a habit, and I encourage my clients and students to always protect themselves. Imagine that the sun's light is illuminating the brightest light around you. Take those lights and swirl them around you like a tornado. Then put yourself inside an egg and close it tightly. The shell of the egg is a mirror, so anything around you that is not positive will go back to where it came from. Then say, "Anything that is in, near, around, or about me that is not of light, go back to where you came from and turn to light if you choose—*but stay away from me!*" No one and nothing has power over you unless you give it to them. Once you protect yourself, you can protect your loved ones in their own mirrored eggs. Always protect yourself first. Then protect your loved ones. The first true love is self-love. It doesn't mean you are selfish; it means your needs matter. Different people use different methods of protection.

Some people pray with the rosary beads. Native Americans use sage to clear the air of any negative spirits. Different religions have different prayers to stay protected. I suggest you find the one that resonates with you. But by all means, it's important to protect ourselves. Prayer is positive thinking. Positive energy attracts positive energy and brings positive results. Unfortunately, negative energy attracts negative energy and brings negative results. So by all means, try to keep the energy positive!

〜〜〜〜〜〜〜〜〜〜

Everything is made up of energy. So when we are familiar with a person or a place, we can pick up on the energy of that person or that place. Mary Helen's daughter was feeling the energy at the school and sensed a problem even if she didn't know exactly what it was. I always say that evil tips us off, and the Universe always tips us off, to protect ourselves. Mary Helen's daughter's story is particularly interesting to me because if she had that premonition, she needs to learn to be more aware of her intuition and her dreams. Some dreams are psychological, but some are prophetic. Many times a prophetic dream may not be about exactly what you are dreaming, but it is symbolic. Because our minds are so busy all day and full of noise, the only time our minds are quiet enough is when we are sleeping. Sometimes that's the only time our guardian angels or spirit guides can get a message to us: through our dreams.

Mary Helen also had recurring dreams of places she hadn't yet visited. She grew up in and later moved back to Sacramento, but she had dreams of being in the desert with skies in hues of purple and orange. When she was sixteen, her family moved to Albuquerque, New Mexico. Shortly after they moved, she was out with some new friends, watching the sunset. The sky was adorned with hues of purple and orange, and she felt like she had been there before. She was in awe because she was actually standing there and experiencing the dream she'd had so many times before. It was so odd to her because she'd had no idea she was going to be moving to the desert when she kept dreaming the same dream.

This feeling is similar to déjà vu, when you feel like you have experienced something before, a familiar feeling like you had been there before but really had not. I always tell people that déjà vu means you are in the right place at the right time. As I was talking to Mary Helen, I recalled a dream that I kept having. In the dream, I have a house on a big lake. I always think it is like the cottage we grew up on in the summers in Michigan. It also makes me wonder whether, if we are constantly dreaming about a certain place, it means we lived there in a past life.

Mary Helen thanked me for building such a great community of people where everyone was supportive of each
other. I feel so blessed to be able to present my podcast and
that we are all learning each week from each other. I told her
how much I appreciated everyone calling in.

Elizabeth, whose brother had the liver transplant, called
in again. Whether it is *CharVision* or a radio or TV show I'm
doing, the phone lines are always extremely busy, so when a
repeat caller is able to get through, I believe it is because something that needed to be resolved the first time wasn't and we
need to devote more time to listening. I say this because it's
important to recognize that learning to listen to your intuition
takes skill and patience. There is a reason why we talk about
healing as a *practice*; it is a constant experience of learning and
listening and working.

None of Elizabeth's stories of premonitions are what we'd
call positive. She had clear premonitions of her two best friends
and her father before they died. She knew they were going to
die. She had the first big one when she was twenty-four. She
kept telling her friend to go to the doctor because she kept having
abnormal cycles; she had a premonition that her friend was
going to die from lung cancer and kept urging her to go. The
friend finally did go to the doctor, and they did a pap smear and
sent the results to her on a little card, telling her that her pap
smear was normal.

Elizabeth kept telling her, "Please go to another doctor and
get another opinion," because she just knew something was
wrong. The friend actually got really upset with Elizabeth.

The friend said, "Stop saying that! You are thinking negatively! You are going to make something bad happen!"

It was a horrible situation, but Elizabeth said, "I just knew!"

About a year later, the doctors found out that Elizabeth's

friend had cervical cancer and it had spread to her lungs. Elizabeth went through the whole radiation and chemo with her friend. When the doctors finally diagnosed the friend as terminal, she came over, sat with Elizabeth, and said, "You were right. I should have listened to your intuition." It was so hard, Elizabeth said, because there was nothing she could do about it! She was the second caller that evening who had known something ahead of time and tried to warn someone. She was just trying to protect her friend.

There's an old saying: "Don't shoot the messenger." People don't want to hear bad news even if it is said with love and to protect and help them. This is why before I do a reading on anyone, I always ask for permission. But then again, it was her friend's life she was trying to save, and she talked about it and had closure. Elizabeth was by her bedside when she passed away.

Later, Elizabeth married and got pregnant with her first child. Her father had been ill her entire childhood and had been in and out of hospitals. She said it was a normal thing for their family. She added, "I never thought all those times, *He's going to die this time.* When I got pregnant, I knew my father was going to pass away before my son was born. My dad was from the old school and didn't like going to doctors. I talked him into seeing his doctors, but they couldn't find anything. My husband and I knew it was going to be a boy and didn't tell anyone, but I told my dad, 'It's a boy, and we are going to name him after you.' My dad passed away just about five weeks before my son was born."

Elizabeth's third premonition was about another very dear friend, Tracey. "Tracey got pregnant, and she had a premonition that her baby had Down syndrome. At the same time, I had the same premonition," said Elizabeth. "We were both afraid to tell each other, and finally, we talked about it." Tracey didn't want to say anything, because she was afraid it would make it real.

Elizabeth continued, "I didn't want to say anything, either, because in the past, people got upset. Tracey went to have an amniocentesis done, because she was forty-three. She came over to my house and was with me when she got the call about the amnio." Elizabeth and Tracey looked at each other, and they just knew without ever saying a word that the baby had Down syndrome.

The thing Elizabeth did not tell Tracey was that she also had a premonition that Tracey would die. Elizabeth was afraid to tell her because of her past experiences when she had warned people and they had blamed her. This time, she didn't know how she could let it pass. Tracey had high blood pressure and frequently did not take her medication for it.

When the baby was about six months old, Tracey's blood pressure got very high, and she told Elizabeth that she had run out of her medicine. Elizabeth said, "Tracey, you have got to promise me that you will go to the ER. You have got to go now." And Tracey said, "Why? Am I going to die?" And Elizabeth said, "I don't think you are going to die, but just promise me you will go, because something bad could really happen." Elizabeth, recounting the story, told me, "We are both nurses, and she knew better."

Tracey didn't go, and she then had a brain aneurysm and died. Elizabeth felt guilty for years after, thinking that maybe she should have told Tracey. All of Elizabeth's premonitions were about illness or death. And in each case, she felt guilty or responsible for sharing or not sharing her concerns.

When I think of the lessons from Elizabeth's stories and why I might be called on to share them, three things come to mind. First, and most important, one of the biggest sources of our "feelings" is from our physical selves, yet think of how many times we dismiss how we physically feel. We are not feeling well, but how often do we ignore it until symptoms worsen? If your body is trying to tell you something, listen!

Second, there is no accounting for how people will receive information. Professionally, people pay me to hear my intuition or my readings, but then they fight with me or dismiss what I am telling them. It is incredible how many times people pay me to do readings and then tell me that I am wrong—that is, when I am telling them what they do not want to hear. It has taken me a long time, and often, I still struggle with the fact that I can say what I say, but it is not my responsibility to make people listen. People hear what they want to hear, and that's okay. It is ultimately not Elizabeth's responsibility to remind her friend to take her medicine, or tell resistant people to go to the doctor or take care of themselves in other ways. Our intuition and spirits are guides; they are not armed soldiers. It is not on us to force people to hear us, but this doesn't stop us from being extremely distressed when others don't take our advice.

This brings me to my third lesson from Elizabeth's story: the power of repetition itself. All of us need to experience something more than once to learn it. Education is not instant. Lessons are difficult because we often have to put in the hard work of failing, picking ourselves back up, and trying again. If you find yourself in the same pattern of doing the same thing over and over again, think about what your intuition might be trying to tell you. Is there something right in front of you that you are refusing to see? The more we can let go of our fears, the closer we will be to our intuitive selves.

We had a repeat caller on *CharVision* named Johanna. Johanna said that when she was a small child, she saw a ghostly hand reaching out for her. She told her sister, who said, "Don't let that hand come after you. It's the hand of death." Years later, Johanna's five-year-old son drowned. When Johanna was pregnant again, her mother started crying. Johanna said this was unusual, as her mother never cried. Johanna asked her mother why she was crying, and her mother said she had a premonition that one of her children was going to die. As soon as her mother spoke the words, Johanna knew her mother was speaking about her sister, Sandra. When Sandra was pregnant, Johanna started gathering little trinkets for her, with protective spiritual prayers like, "May the Lord protect you." While Johanna was visiting, she said, "Sandy, let's make a pact. If you die first, you find a way to come tell me. If I die, I will come tell you." Johanna said she just knew, she had no doubt that her sister was going to die. Sandy gave birth to her son and passed away two years later. There is such a thing as mother's intuition. The day their mother started crying, seemingly for no reason, it was because her feeling that one of her children was going to die was accurate. One of the most tragic events is when a child dies before their parents. I would never presume to understand that pain or sadness. I have, however, been blessed to have experiences where I have been able to pass on messages from a child to their parent, and the messages are almost always filled with love and gratitude.

Johanna told us about her mother-in-law, who had cancer. In those years, they didn't know as much about cancer as they do now. One day, her mother-in-law was in the hospital and feeling great. The doctors and the family all thought the medicine was doing its job and that she would recover. That night, Johanna said, her husband, Robert, had a dream about his mother and told Johanna his mother was going to be fine! In the dream, he said he could only see his mother's feet, and she kept saying,

"Robert, Robert, I'm okay. I'm okay." As Robert spoke, Johanna had an overwhelming feeling that her mother-in-law was going to die that day. She begged her husband not to go to work. She remembered saying, "Please don't go to work! Don't go to work." Robert was so confident from his dream, he said, "No, it's fine, my mother is going to be fine." As soon as he got to work, which was an hour away, his mother passed.

Johanna stopped paying attention to her feelings because other people told her it was the devil's work. I told Johanna it is not the devil's work unless someone is using their abilities to manipulate or hurt others. As in every profession, there are honest and dishonest people. When someone with an intuitive gift is pure of heart and lives with a conscience, unless they are being fooled, the information they share will be healing and helpful. As I have mentioned, that's why I say a prayer with every single one of my clients before I read for them and make sure the messages I'm getting are from the highest place of goodness, love, and God. I told Johanna that she was pure and her messages were coming from a place of healing, even if the messages were to prepare someone for a loved one's passing. She was trying to save her husband from going through the grief of not being at the hospital with his mother, or at least nearby, instead of having to drive an hour back, grieving. Another time, Robert got cancer, and Johanna knew he would be fine—and he was. I told Johanna that every time she had a premonition, it was her spirit guides helping her to try to prevent a problem. She did not have to be afraid of her intuition, because it was coming from a place of love and healing.

A young man from Michigan named Colby called next. Colby said that when he was growing up, he had been super close to his grandmother. He would see her every day, and they were always very connected. His childhood was a little tumultuous because his parents had divorced when he was young.

Although he loved his parents, his solid support system was his grandmother. She was like a second mother to him and helped him get through all the changes at home.

Colby was a student at Arizona State and came home to Michigan for the summer. One year, he spent the summer helping his grandmother around the house. She passed away that August. She was completely independent and did not show her age at all. Her death was a shock for everyone. She'd had a premonition a month before she passed; a vivid dream in which she saw her mom and her sister, who had already passed away. The dream was so real that she'd thought she had died. In the dream, her sister had said to her, "Why are you so scared? Go hug our mother. She wants to see you!" So Colby's grandma had gone and hugged her mother, who kept saying in an excited voice, "Come on! Come join the party!" The grandmother had said, "No, no, please just let me go back and get ready."

The dream gave me goose bumps. I told Colby his grandmother had told him the dream so both of them could prepare.

He said, "Char, it was insane! My grandmother was religious but also had an issue because she liked to be in control. Just seeing her let go was incredible."

She didn't tell anyone about the dream except for Colby and her sister, Colby's great-aunt. She didn't want to talk about it because she thought she was going to die. She was completely healthy! No one expected it! He said it was crazy how it all worked. He had been spending a lot of time with her, and he could feel her energy being a little different. He would go home, stay with his mom, and tell her, "Look, I'm getting really nervous about Oma!" The way she was talking, Colby felt something was really off.

A couple of nights before she passed, Colby was lying in bed, trying to fall asleep, and he had this image of himself at her funeral, speaking in front of her casket. He looked back and saw her lying in the casket. I told him he was being psychologically prepared. He completely felt that. He was actually with her the moment she passed away. He was with her every step of the way, just like she was with him during his life. He saw that vision, and he couldn't handle it. He kept telling himself it was just his anxiety. But the vision was so real! He saw himself next to the casket, which was a little bit unique. He told me he saw the color of it and everything!

Colby said he always felt pretty connected to his angels and had always been interested in the spirit world. He said feathers were his sign, and anytime he ever doubted anything or asked for a sign or verification, he would find a feather, and that would tell him everything would be okay. The morning his grandmother passed, his cousin sent him a chart of feathers telling him what they meant. That morning, he went to help his grandmother, and she was on the riding mower. As he got out of the car, he found a blue feather. It caught his eye, so he took a picture of it and sent it to his cousin. From that moment on, the dominoes fell. I said, "I know your grandmother will always watch over you, and you know the sign for her is a feather." He said he talked to her every day. It gave him comfort and trust of what happened in the hereafter. I said, "Your grandma is not there all the time, but she is there a lot!" What a beautiful young man!

Psychic Main Points

* The Universe speaks in signs, symbols, and feelings.
* As evidenced by the stories, when you listen to the language of the Universe, you will be tuned in to life itself.

   ⁕ We can feel the energy and communicate to those here, and those who have gone on beyond.

Psychic Journal Practice

Get your I AM PSYCHIC Journal.
  Do the following exercises:

   ⁕ You wanted something. Maybe it was a business deal or romance and you had a gut feeling not to do it, but your emotions got in the way and you did it anyway. You suffered the consequences. Time proved that your first impression was correct.

   ⁕ Make a list of the times you didn't listen to your intuition.

   ⁕ Make a list of times when you did listen to your intuition and avoided a problem.

   ⁕ Make a list of your thoughts. Are your thoughts mostly positive or negative?

     → Positive energy attracts positive energy, and negative energy attracts negative energy. When you live with faith and positive energy, it is easy to be more aware of a warning in your life.

   ⁕ Do you have the four Cs—the courage to own your intuition, the confidence to use it, the willingness to commit yourself to focusing on it, and most of all the courage to conquer and act upon your feelings? Make a list of times you acted upon your feelings.

   ⁕ We use our other five senses along with emotional feelings to enhance our sixth sense. Some spirits visit by evoking a smell, such as your grandfather's pipe smoke or your mother's perfume. You may get goose bumps as validation of a confirmed psychic feeling. You may taste something that reminds you of a loved one.

⟶ Make a list of times you knew you had a visitation from a deceased loved one.

✳ Do you remember your dreams? Deceased loved ones like to visit us when our minds are quiet, usually while we're sleeping. The visitations seem very real. There is usually a message in such a dream. Many times, the message is symbolic.

⟶ Make a list of the times you had a visitation in a dream.

✳ Make a list of times that you had an "all-knowing feeling" that went against all logic but was correct!

✳ Do you make choices with a clear conscience? Write down times you went against your better judgment.

✳ Many of our beloved pets that have passed over will visit us. A lot of times, they will scoot by in our peripheral vision. Has this happened to you?

7

FOLLOW YOUR GUT

~~~~~~~~~~~~~~~~~~~~~~~~~~~~~~~~~~~~

What you will learn in this chapter: This chapter may seem similar to others, but it's nuanced in the way that being psychic is nuanced. Listening to your intuition is key, and you'll see examples here of those who did and did not follow their intuition. Pay close attention, and key into your own intuition as you read the chapter.

~~~~~~~~~~~~~~~~~~~~~~~~~~~~~~~~~~~~

I asked my viewers to tell me about times they listened to their psychic intuitive sense and the times they did not listen and what the results were.

I told my viewers I was doing a reading for a client and I could tell that the veil between here and the spirit world was much thinner and easier to connect to than usual. I told them that earlier in the week, I had taken a nap and had a vivid dream about my deceased mother. She told me she was sick, but Katherine—the woman who helped raise me as a child and, later in life, helped care for my mother in her old age— was staying upstairs and taking care of her. I knew my mother was trying to tell me something, but I didn't know what. I called both my sisters to see if they had any ideas. That same night, when I went to sleep, I again had a vivid dream about my mother, who told me she had cancer. Our mother never had cancer, so I knew this was a message for our family. My mother was trying to either prevent a problem or send a message, but I didn't know what! You would think as a psychic and her daughter, I would be better at knowing, but unfortunately that's not how it works, or at least not how it works for me. All I can do is stay open and alert so that when the time comes, I can recognize the signs early if it's a warning and work toward a positive conclusion. Not all dreams are warnings. As I thought about it, I realized that within those last two years two very close relatives to me had Stage 1 breast cancer. They are now both cancer-free. My mother might have been telling me that she and Katherine were watching over them. I have noticed, in the last fifty years of doing this work, that there are definitely times when the veil between heaven and Earth is much thinner, but I don't know why. I would love to find out. I believe that when people come to us in dreams, it's not literal but symbolic. The pieces are there, but it's a puzzle we need to figure out. Unfortunately, we sometimes let our fears chime in first. Many of us think the dreams are only warnings. They are not always a warning. Much of the time they are messages saying, *I am here watching over you. I protected you.*

Many times, we learn how important our intuition is because of a time when we *didn't* listen to it. The intuitive feeling comes subtly. It's not like a booming, deep voice of God comes to you. You may be in the busiest part of your day and something says to call your child, call your mother, or call your friend; even though it inconveniences you, you follow through, and it turns out you were needed. The reason that we need to learn from this is because the next time, it could be a matter of life and death. You are about to board an airplane for a business trip, and your gut tells you not to go. Then you argue with yourself because you have an important business meeting and you don't have a "rational" reason not to go. It's a real dilemma when these intuitive feelings happen; however, we need to understand that these feelings are here to protect us. We have all heard stories of people not taking a flight at the last minute, not getting in the car, or the opposite—making a trip or giving someone a call, and being grateful for the rest of their lives that they listened to their intuition and avoided tragedy or gained something priceless through a last-minute decision. Why do we go against our gut feelings? Most of the time, it is because we let our emotions or fears get in the way.

Marci called in. She has been talking to me for fifteen years, and we tease each other about who loves who more. Marci described how she had been in a taxi in New York City, and as soon as she got in the cab, she felt a bad vibe. During her cab ride, she and the driver got stuck on the left side of a major highway, and it was extremely dangerous. She said after that, she always tried to listen to her intuition. A couple of years ago, she thought she was going to be in a car accident and later ended up getting in one. She had a reading with me after that, and I got mad at her because she didn't work at preventing it from happening; she is so much more aware of her intuition now. She asked me to read for her, and I saw her moving to San Diego. I asked if she had earthquake insurance, because I was concerned about an earthquake along the coast of California.

The next caller was Denise from Michigan, another client of mine. She went to her doctor because she had a fever. Her doctor wasn't able to see anything wrong, so he sent her to a local hospital close to her home. The first night at the hospital,

Denise called her doctor at two o'clock in the morning and said, "I don't know if you believe in intuition, but I can't stay at this hospital."

He said, "Oh, you'll be fine."

She said, "No! Something bad is gonna happen. I want to leave." She then lied and said she had a dog she had to take care of. The hospital administration wouldn't let her leave. Well, she almost died twice while she was there! They had to wash her insides out because her appendix had been burst for four days but she didn't know because she didn't have any pain.

Afterward, Denise went back to her own room from the recovery room. Then she had a very vivid dream about her deceased parents. They were at the airport. Her parents had their luggage and their tickets, and they were not saying anything. She was having trouble with the ticketing agent. She told the agent that someone had stolen her luggage and she didn't have her boarding pass. "Here's my license. Please just reissue my boarding pass," she said. "My parents are old and sick. I have to take care of them. I have to take them home." In her dream, the ticketing agent argued with her and wouldn't issue her a new boarding pass.

At that moment in the dream, all the machines in her hospital room went off. Her heart rate had dropped precariously low—in the forties—and her oxygen level had dipped below ninety. She thought, *I have to stay awake. If not, I will die.* Then she remembered the reading I'd given her some time back. She thought, *Char told me I would live for a good long while, and I'm not going to die this year.* Nobody came when all her alarms went off. She kept concentrating on surviving and getting her vitals in balance. She later told the story to my sister Alicia, who said, "Denise, that's one of the times you almost died."

On the call, I told Denise she sounded good and I was glad she was working with Alicia, who kept checking up on her. While in the recovery room, she had a dream in which she said goodbye to all her relatives in Italy. She was speaking to all her relatives in Italian, which she doesn't speak well. Alicia told her, "That's the other time you almost died." Denise's positive attitude and faith kept her alive. I told her how honored I was that she thought of me at a time that she was facing life and death. I was blown away by that!

Denise returned to her family doctor a couple of days after she got out of the hospital, because she was having complications from the procedure. When she went to her follow-up, she told her doctor, "I'm sorry I had to wake you up at two o'clock in the morning, but my intuition told me I couldn't stay at that hospital, and I almost died." The doctor still didn't believe her!

When she went back to him for her six-week checkup, he said, "You know, you almost died."

She said, "I almost died *twice*! When I tell you something, it's like I know already!" She thought the doctor was finally becoming a believer!

I want to take a moment here to point out how important it is to advocate for your health—when you "feel" something is off, don't let yourself be dismissed. Unfortunately, there is a long history of gender bias against women in health care. According to a Duke University study, more than one half of women report their health concerns were dismissed or ignored by a provider. **When your intuition is telling you that you don't "feel right," listen—and if necessary, fight to be heard.** Don't let your intuition be ignored!

Later in my call with Denise, I picked up on the names

Marie and *Joseph*. The middle name of Denise's deceased sister is Marie, and the middle name of her father is Joseph. I told her they were both with her. They were together. (People don't realize that when I read for others, I don't remember what I say.) I told Denise she was protected and she was okay. She knew it. She just wanted to reiterate to the listeners that when you get a strong intuitive feeling, you should act on it! She knew that hospital was not a good place for her, but they wouldn't let her leave. She got really upset and said she was never going back to that hospital again. The next time she had to be readmitted, she went to a different hospital. She said, "Can you imagine telling my doctor my intuition told me not to stay at the hospital? He must have thought I was nuts!" We laughed about it after the fact, but again, I urge you, listen to your intuition!

The next caller made my day. Bernie and his wife, Laurie, said they had become big fans of mine and looked forward to watching my show every Friday night! (When I started *Char-Vision*, I didn't expect much. I said I would have been happy if we'd had five people watching. Now we have thousands!) Bernie is a good storyteller. He has a great New York accent and reminds me of what a "tough guy" on TV sounds like when he speaks. Bernie said Laurie had a ticket to LA on American Airlines Flight 11 out of Logan International Airport on 9/11. They had a big fight. He had a gut feeling and said, "Honey, I really don't want you to go. You can go on the trip, but just change your ticket." Laurie finally gave in and moved her ticket. On 9/11, Bernie was getting his meat delivery van fixed at a shop near Logan International. He climbed onto the roof of the building. He was into tai chi, and there's a form called *holding up the sky*. At that moment, Bernie sent healing, loving energy to all the planes in the sky on 9/11! This was before the terrorist attacks happened that day. Amazing!

Bernie has now become a spiritualist and gets most of his messages in precognitive dreams. One night, he had a dream about a priest, and a priest ended up moving into the house across the street from them. He had a dream about me where I grabbed him by the lapel and said, "I love you." The next day, he went to the Unitarian Universalist church, and in the middle of the service, they said, "Turn to the person next to you and say, 'I love you.'" Last year, he dreamed he was ordering supplies for a hospital ship. He was standing in front of a medicine cabinet, writing down what he needed. All of a sudden, he ended up on deck. He wrote 23 in black marker on a life jacket. He thinks he is going to get the answers for the coronavirus soon.

Bernie also uses a dream moods dictionary. He had a dream about a man on a bicycle who had his leg up in the air; the man was wearing a red jogging suit and a bike helmet and had long hair. Later, Bernie went to a spiritualist church in Cape Cod, Massachusetts, and the reader asked if anyone could accept a man who lost his leg to shrapnel. Bernie felt it was the bicycling man from his dream, who had lost one of his legs in Vietnam. Bernie felt it was his spirit guide that was in his dream on the bike.

Bernie started drinking in 1995. His guide died of alcoholism, and the reason he was helping Bernie was to get him to stop drinking. He was pulling for him from the other side. I told him that I found that people I knew who were recovered alcoholics were extremely intuitive and sensitive. They were fighting the demons and were now very intuitive. It always made me think that the dark side was trying to keep them from using their natural healing intuition. The darkness tried to take the good people like Bernie, who were pure and caring and loving, to stop them from living healthy lives. He said that was what he got from my book—that low-level energies would try to attach themselves to a person. He said, "You have to keep your thoughts positive and clean so you can act with the higher levels of energies."

Once when Bernie was driving in his meat delivery van, he had the thought: *Don't go through that green light.* He thought, *I can't just stop at a green light.* Meanwhile, someone ran a red light on the cross street while Bernie coasted toward the intersection. He felt his nanna protected him. But his question was, who was trying to kill him?

Bernie also does table tipping. I told him to be very careful doing that. Table tipping is what they do in séances. People sit around with their fingertips on the tabletop. All of a sudden, the table starts vibrating, and spirits communicate from it. Bernie is convinced that he has a big angel, but I know it is still dangerous to do. He's a physical medium, and that means his energy can move objects like the table. I'm still very leery of doing that, even though he is convinced his prayers protect him. I have personally found that it welcomes more lower entities on it and can fool you. I told him that when I first started mediumship, I was involved with a trance medium who did table tipping. Low-level energies will try to come in on the physical medium stuff. I won't touch that. As I have written and told him, it's kind of like the Ouija board. It will tell a kid nine accurate things, and the tenth instruction will be to build a bomb and blow up their school. That's how tricksters work. Bernie thinks if you do spiritual house cleaning and call on God it's sometimes okay. He says he does it to prove the continuity of life so people know they have a soul and are playing the big game, that we are playing for keeps.

Bernie almost got abducted when he was five years old, when a man tried to lure him into his apartment by saying he had puppies. The man said, "Go onto that balcony over there." Bernie saw an evil expression come over the guy's face, and Bernie closed his eyes and did a backflip off that balcony to get away from the man. He cleared the railing behind him. He felt that God saved him. He asked for a sign about that experience. I told him when he goes to the spiritualist church, he should read for some of the people. He said one of the mediums already dragged him up there to do just that.

Wanda moved to Washington, D.C., for a job. She didn't know anyone and decided to take a walk to get her hair done. As she approached the Potomac River, she came to a bridge, and something told her not to cross and to go back to her hotel. She turned around and noticed a man following behind her. He stopped and said, "Where are you going?" Wanda told him she wanted to go get her hair done, and as she was speaking, she saw him look at her purse. That confirmed her decision to not cross that bridge, and she turned back. The craziest story Wanda shared was that once, in the 1970s, when she was only fourteen, she and her sisters were driving through Alabama and a guy in a yellow car tried to pick them up. They remembered what he looked like and what he drove. A few years later, they saw him on the news. It was Ted Bundy!

Psychic Main Points

* ⁎ Be aware of your dreams.
* ⁎ Try to decipher whether your dream is psychological or psychic.

* Don't ignore a divine message given to you.
* Have the courage to listen and act upon your insight.

Psychic Journal Practice

Get your I AM PSYCHIC Journal.
Answer these questions:

* What are some examples of dreams you have had that have guided you?
* What results did you have after being guided by your dreams?
* How did you interpret your psychic messages?
* How many times were you inconvenienced by an intuitive message but were later grateful that you acted upon it and followed through?
* What questions did the messages answer?

8

LOVE IS THE BRIDGE

〜〜〜〜〜〜〜〜〜〜〜〜〜〜〜〜〜〜〜〜〜〜〜〜

What you will learn in this chapter: Love is the key for psychics to have clear experiences. To get the strongest and most clear messages from life, an intuitive needs to not only release and let go (as previously discussed) but to also embrace all of life with love. Love transcends our egos. Stay in love, don't judge, and you will be able to be a beacon of light for life, to yourself, and to others.

〜〜〜〜〜〜〜〜〜〜〜〜〜〜〜〜〜〜〜〜〜〜〜〜

I have been taping *CharVision* since 2015. People need a place to gather where there are others they resonate with. People are looking for communities where they have an interest and can communicate with each other about what they have in common, not just about the spiritual world but about many different subjects—holism and health, frontline workers for COVID, and loving animals, to name a few. I do intuition retreats, and I have two clients who come to my retreat who love you and who have a validation story for you. John Edward is a colleague and friend. He was a guest on *CharVision*. I had known that he helped these sisters and had them call in. Sylvia shared her experience:

Thirteen years ago at the Los Angeles Millennium hotel, I was among several hundred people hoping to get a reading at John Edward's event. I was lucky enough to have my mother-in-law come through to John, and she brought information about our mother's family. John said, "They're saying that your mother was one of six," and I said, "No, she was one of five, but that's okay! Keep going!"

And he said, "No, they're saying one of six. Just remember that and look into it."

We asked our mother, and she said no, there were only five siblings—no adoptions, no foster children, no one else. Finally, we asked our aunt, and she told us that her mother had lost her first child. He was born full-term but only lived a few hours. Our grandmother was devastated, and it was *never* spoken of in the family—except that many years later she did tell her youngest daughter, our aunt. With our aunt's confirmation, it still took us ten years to find the birth and death certificates and a grave. We finally found the grave marker for our grandparents' first child, who was born and died on June 17, 1910, in Eden, New York.

Sylvia and her sister Barbara had a plaque made. The last name was Booth. So it read: BABY BOOTH BORN AND DIED JUNE 17, 1910. It kept bugging them to do something to help put the baby to rest, and it took them ten years to do it, but it was really satisfying.

The family was not comfortable revealing something like this at the time, and Barbara and Sylvia think their grandmother was riddled with guilt. They had a farm and watched calves being born all the time, so their grandmother thought that because she could deliver calves and foals she could deliver this baby on her own. But when the baby was born with a cord around his neck, she didn't know what to do. She didn't call the doctor in time. She was so upset that it was too painful to tell anyone, including her children, about it. He wasn't in the family Bible or named. No one else alive on the planet knew anything about this but Barbara and Sylvia's ninety-year-old aunt. It meant a lot for them to do this and take it back to their aunt and tell her there was a baby! John said those miscarriages and stillborns are still energetically around us. He thought it was so cool. The sisters believed in his reading so much that they went out of their way to validate it, and it helped them find closure.

The ironic thing is that it's called the Eden Evergreen cemetery. There's so much synchronicity.

They said that I always told them that **love is the bridge that connects us to each other and the spirit world.** When there's love among people, it never dies, so all those relationships from the past brought them together.

~~~~~~~~~~~~~~~~~~

CHAR TIP:
LOVING WHAT NEEDS
TO BE LOVED

Take a few breaths and relax. Allow yourself to be open to what life wants to show you.

In your I AM PSYCHIC Journal, make a list of those experiences and/or people that you believe need more love. These don't have to be experiences or people that you "agree" with, and you offering love doesn't condone inappropriateness. Just make the list without judging it.

Take a breath when you are finished.

Now look over the list, and for each experience/person, say this affirmation (or one similar): "May you be enveloped in the light of love."

If there are experiences/people that you don't feel comfortable doing this with, leave them for now without judging yourself. Love yourself for being willing to extend love, even when and where it's uncomfortable to do so.

Take another breath and say, "Love is my compass. I release all that is unlike love."

Watch how doing this practice not only extends love to others but also brings more love into your life.

~~~~~~~~~~~~~~~~

Barbara said in her first reading that I figured out that she and Sylvia were half sisters. Their fathers were brothers. Their mother had married one of the brothers, and after he crossed over, she married the other. They were worried, and I said, "No, it's fine. They are all together! They all still have the love that they had for each other. They did love each other at different times and in different ways, but that's the glue that holds them together." The interesting thing about the cemetery was that her grandfather purchased six plots when he was going to bury the baby. They never used them, so they were handed down, and now Sylvia has five plots in the Eden Evergreen Cemetery. She said, "That's where I'm going."

Then Sylvia brought up the time when they were at my retreat in Palm Springs. She had told me she was a Frank Sinatra fan. They tried to go find his grave that day, but the cemetery was closed. I piled us in the car at ten o'clock at night and said, "I have a feeling we can get into the cemetery." We drove to a different gate, with me leading us in the song "High Hopes," and somehow the gate was open! We have the pictures to prove it. We knew Sinatra was buried next to Sonny Bono and Hoagy Carmichael. After going through the gate, we wondered where the grave would be. It was pitch-black, but we had cell phones and flashlights. "We literally walked about ten feet and boom! There it was, right in front of us!" Sylvia concluded.

John liked the Frank Sinatra cemetery story, because it was like I was taking them on a field trip teaching how to follow your intuition. I was glad that John had introduced Sylvia and Barb to me, and I'm so happy it came full circle!

Later in the show, Barbara from Michigan called. She said she'd heard a voice, but how could you tell if it was real? John said he used the 95 percent to 5 percent rule. He pushed the experience away to a point where he asked himself, *Okay, am I just thinking that? Or is it being given to me?* He told her, "The fact that you are questioning it is good! Five percent of the time, it's an actual connection or the information is actually coming through."

CHAR TIP: DISCOVERING YOUR PATTERNS

There's always a pattern with your intuition, and this will help you to determine what is "real" versus what is your mind making things up. **Patterns get established whether it is in the physical world or the spiritual world.** Sometimes you may find feathers or lights flickering songs on the radio, or 11–11. It's like a thought that's not your own. So when you get a sign or feel something, it's good to journal and ask questions for validation of what you received.

Try this:

When you feel something or see a sign, write it down in your journal, along with the date and time.

Next, in your journal, ask life for validation and write that down.

Pay attention to see what is true and what isn't. This will help you to see the intuitive patterns you experience.

~~~~~~~~~~~~~~~~~~~~

One of my students often writes down such signs, and there are times the handwriting doesn't look like hers. It sounds like automatic writing, where people allow their angels and spirit guides to come through them to pass along messages. There was a famous journalist named Ruth Montgomery who worked for *The Washington Post*. She was assigned to write an article about the medium Arthur Ford. She said, "I'm not doing this! I'm a hard-core journalist! I'm not writing about BS medium stuff." Well, she had to do the article. She did it, and it changed her life. She developed her abilities and did automatic typing. After Arthur Ford died, she would channel him, and he would come through.

At the time of this writing, it's been ten months of quarantine for me now in Palm Springs, California. The summer is hot in the desert. Some days were 120 degrees. I only went out in the morning and evening. It's December now, and the holidays are around the corner. The fruit trees are in bloom again, and I've been picking Meyer lemons when I'm cooking. They are delicious. I keep in touch with my family and friends. My precious Chihuahua Sunny keeps me company, and we go for a walk every morning. I'm blessed to read for my clients and air *CharVision* every Friday evening.

Recently on my show, I asked people to call in if they had

ever had a near-death experience or were pronounced dead and came back to life. I asked how this experience affected their psychic abilities. Most people who have a near-death experience have a euphoric feeling, and many do not want to come back to the Earth plane. However, some people don't always go to a wonderful place. It depends on their karma. I told the story about when I was on *Dr. Oz* and there were a few people who'd had NDEs. Two of the experiences were beautiful. One woman was in Lake Michigan drowning, and she heard her fiancé's voice praying for her. As beautiful as the spirit world was, she knew she had more lessons on Earth, and the love of her soon-to-be husband brought her back.

However, one man had an unpleasant experience. He was an atheist and didn't believe in a higher divine being. When he died, he was in a dark place. He saw demons and was in horrific pain. It also had the worst odor you could imagine. For once in his life, he called out to God, and Jesus Christ came to him. Christ told him that he would take him out of his suffering, but he needed to be kinder, more loving, and believe in God. The man was sent back to Earth. His lifeless body was regenerated, and he lived the rest of his life with a great faith in God and a kinder attitude.

Psychic Main Points

* Love is supreme to all other emotions.
* Pay attention to how you receive information; use your I AM PSYCHIC Journal to document your intuition.
* Use the divine God energy (or however you identify it) to connect to your higher self.
* Karma is real.

Psychic Journal Practice

Get your I AM PSYCHIC Journal.

Spend a day, or several days if possible, writing down your intuitions, your signs, your feelings. Always include a date and time. Every day, look at what you wrote, and follow up when you feel so moved.

Keep a running list of those feelings/intuitions/signs that proved to be true. Remember, some of your intuitive experiences will happen quickly, and some will take days, weeks, months, or occasionally even years to come to fruition.

Pay attention to those things that don't come to fruition.

9

NEAR-DEATH EXPERIENCES

What you will learn in this chapter: We briefly covered near-death experiences in the previous chapter, and in this chapter, we'll take a deeper dive into this phenomenon. Notice the lessons that NDEs offer, and see what speaks to you the most.

We had a caller who'd had surgery for her spine. It had been difficult for her to come out of the anesthesia. She remembered coming out of it in the recovery room in the hospital. She was in extreme, unmanageable pain. She wanted painkillers. The nurses wouldn't give them to her because they would make her go back to sleep, and she needed to stay awake. She tried to focus. She was at a point where she grabbed the nurses and begged them to let her die. She is not a quitter, but it was too excruciating. She was ready to give up. The nurse said, "I can't do that." So she started meditating, thinking she should do something different. She needed to distract herself from the pain. In her meditation, she imagined herself on the beach. All of a sudden, the pain started to disappear. She felt like she was partially out of her body. She looked toward her legs, because she was paralyzed, and saw what appeared to be flashing angels. The pain was gone. The angels told her telepathically that they were there to help her. When they touched her legs, a spark would enter the limb. When the angels left, she was back and in horrific pain again and was yelling for the nurses to get her out of there. She remembered doctors working on her and going crazy all around her. They were panicking because she'd bled during the surgery and had lost a lot of blood, and she was physically restrained. When the angels had been talking to her telepathically, the pain had vanished. When she saw the angels again, she felt like she'd sat up and watched them, even though it was impossible. She knew she wasn't hallucinating, because they would not give her anything to relieve the pain. It took her months to recuperate. She went into a rehabilitation facility, where she was abused. Someone hit her and gave her a black eye. She heard a voice say, "If you don't get out of here today, you will never make it." She called 911, and they rescued her from the facility. She thanked me for helping her son and her family. I told her she was going to be a grandmother, and at the time I gave her the reading, she didn't know her daughter was pregnant.

The next caller was Fran. In 1992, she was in a terrible car accident that left her disabled. Her seat belt failed, her head hit the window, and she was ejected into the road, where she flatlined. Her heart stopped working, and she could hear them talking about giving her treatments. They were doing everything they could to help her. As that was happening, the essence of her grandmother took her over; Fran had no doubt that it was her. Like a broken record, her grandma kept saying, "It's okay. You'll be fine!" She was thrilled to hear from her loved one, but it got so monotonous and annoying! There was no white light. It was like a standstill, but she was enveloped in the essence of her grandmother. It was beautiful!

Then her SA node stopped, and her heart kicked in on its own. Her body had restarted its own heart. Everyone has an atrial node. It's like a backup generator. Sometimes it kicks in and takes over, and sometimes not. Fran was blessed that hers took over. She lived with her parents for the next few years. She was miserable and sick, and when her parents were not looking, she sometimes had to crawl up the stairs. She didn't want them to see how bad she was. It was so hard for her because she is well educated and likes to work. But after a few years, her grandmother's words came back to her and she thought, *You are okay now!* It was true. She's all better now.

Fran also had a second NDE. When her mom passed away unexpectedly, Fran felt like the wind was taken out of her sails. Then her dad got terribly sick. She didn't even have time to grieve her mother. When she finally could, she lost it. She hyperventilated and dropped to her knees, dry-heaving over the toilet. She knew she was in trouble. It seemed like it went on forever. As much as she tried, Fran couldn't catch her breath. She thought that if she died, no one would find her for days. Then her dog started jumping on her. Her dog actually saved her; her dog healed her. The energy of a dog's unconditional love is powerful! I asked how these experiences affected her psychic abilities. She said, "Nothing else matters! Family, friends, love, kindness, and goodness. That's all that matters."

Sally called in to talk about something that had happened more than sixty years earlier. Her sister, who had been sick, had passed away and was pronounced dead. Her sister saw a tunnel and a white light, then all of a sudden, she was being pulled back, even though she didn't want to return to the Earth plane.

She came back into her physical body and woke up. Their dad was watching over her, crying. Sally's sister knew then that there was a God and tried to explain how important life was. Her sister started understanding the energy of intuition and spirit communication. She said no one talked about it then, because people would think you were crazy. (Some people still feel that way.) Her sister became more aware and intuitive and also opened the family's minds to their own psychic abilities. The whole family was intuitive and understood the process more after her sister's experience.

Deana called about her mother's near-death experience. Her mother had crossed over twenty-five years earlier. During the last five years of her life, she was very sick with COPD and had many respiratory issues. Two years before she died, she went into a respiratory arrest situation. She had been rushed to the hospital. She saw herself being worked on. Her spirit hovered over her body, and she watched the doctors and nurses trying to save her. She still felt pain at that point, but a little later, she felt the pain leave her body. She then went toward a warm, loving light. She described it to Deana as a walkway lined on both sides by people who knew her. Deana said her mom couldn't tell her who they were now, but she was really happy to see them. As she was going toward the light, she heard what seemed to be music, too, but she had no words to describe it, as it was like no other sound she had ever heard before. As she continued along, she felt so much love and warmth surrounding her! She was just so happy! She said she had never been that happy and peaceful in her life. It was the most wonderful feeling. As she was going toward that light, a crab crossed her path (Deana's Zodiac sign is Cancer). She said, "My daughter Deana needs me," and—*bam!*—she went back into her body. She didn't talk to Deana for six weeks after she came out of the hospital! She was very angry with Deana because she brought her back!

It fascinated me that Deana's mother knew the people in the tunnel and was overjoyed to see them but could not explain who they were. I told her they were probably her guardian angels and spirit guides, which Deana also assumed. Her mother remembered that they were people who loved her and were happy to see her, and she felt so welcome. Deana kept phoning her mother, saying, "I know you are back from the hospital. Please call me!" When her mother told Deana why she was angry, Deana said, "I understand, but I'm so glad you are back!"

Before her mother went through this experience, she was very worried about dying and the pain she would feel when she died. When she came back, she never, ever had another worry about dying. Her experience took every bit of fear away! I asked if she became more intuitive and psychic and when she forgave Deana. Deana's mother first had to get well, and at about the six-week point, she just understood that her daughter needed her, loved her, and wanted her back. Deana wasn't ready to let her go yet. Her mom was always an intuitive and empathic person, and her experience definitely enhanced all of that. She had a confidence in her faith and a confidence that everything was going to be okay—and she was ready for it! She was ready to go, but stayed on Earth for her children. It was the ultimate feeling of peace.

People always talked about homecoming, and the way her mom described it felt exactly like that! When her mother first described her experience, her face lit up! There was so much joy in her expression and her entire being. The love and healing surrounding her was euphoric. She remembered that when she came back into her body, the doctors were gone. No one was there. They thought that she had died. They were getting ready to take her body away. Her mother was not a person to make up stories, so it helped Deana with her faith and understanding of the spirit world and life after death. Her mother was straightforward, honest, practical, and factual. She lived in reality.

All of us have a physical body and an ethereal body. There is a silver thread that connects the physical body to the ethereal body, and you never want that silver thread to break.

Two years later, Deana's mother finally crossed over. It was difficult for Deana. They had been so very close. Her mom knew she and her dad needed her with them. Deana and her father became upset hearing her mother cry as the hospital staff tried to put in a PICC line so she could go home instead of staying at the hospital, hooked up to all the medicines. Then Deana and her father would start crying, too. It was absolutely horrible. But her mom was determined to go home. Deana said, like so many other people, it's so hard to let go. So she made a bargain with God to bring her mother back to her. She thought, *Please bring her back*. On one level, Deana just wasn't ready to let her go.

A year later, Deana had to go for an MRI, and they put ink in a vein that wasn't supposed to be used, and it almost exploded the vein. Then they pulled the needle out and put another one in the other arm. As she was put into the MRI machine, she had to be very quiet, but she was feeling the pain from where the vein almost exploded. It was there that she decided if she had to have her mom come back, knowing this pain herself and what she must have gone through, that she loved her mother so much she would have never wanted her to go through pain like that. She was finally able to release her. I told her that when we love someone so much and their bodies are ready to go, it's an unselfish gesture to let them go. It's hard, but it's humane.

Tony, my dear friend and gifted engineer, spoke up about his grandfather Floyd, who had a near-death experience. In 1967, Floyd, a minister and a business owner, died in the hospital and came back to share his story. This was before anyone talked about these experiences. He said he saw the bright light and came out into an open field and that it was beautiful, just beautiful. There was a river, and he saw his mother on the other side. She said, "Floyd, it's not your time, so you must go back." Floyd then heard his wife calling his name. He lived another thirteen years. From the stories Tony heard, this experience changed his grandfather. Floyd was always a good man, but he became more of a giving man. He always treated everyone so well. If someone was alone or without at Christmas or Thanksgiving, he would invite them over. But Tony remembered his grandpa ended up getting lung cancer because he smoked five packs of cigarettes a day. Tony remembered being in his father's grocery store, and his grandfather said, "Tony, I am going into the hospital, and I'm not coming back. I want you to know I love you and be a good boy." He was so calm and confident saying these words. He wasn't scared. It did change him.

Bernie called again to share another experience he'd had. When he was twenty-one, his roommate was head of the Boys' Club in Cambridge, Massachusetts. During a fundraiser one night, he pulled up to the front door of a bar, looking angry, and Bernie followed him in. Some guy had stolen twenty dollars, and his roommate and a bunch of others ended up in a big fight. Five people were stabbed. It was horrific. They all ended up at Cambridge Hospital. Bernie had been stabbed in the leg, and his roommate, who was in the room next door, had been stabbed in the heart. Then Bernie and his friend were in a white light, and there was a man talking to him mentally, saying, "Everything is going to be all right."

Jeanine called about seeing numbers in patterns, like 11–11. When people see 11–11, it means there's synchronicity in your world of energy. A lot of people see that, and it's good luck. It's always a good idea to make a wish when you see that. She makes a wish when she sees those numbers are on her phone. (So do I.)

Jeanine sees spirits all the time. I asked if she had a *J* initial around her, and I got the name *James*—her brother. Then I asked who John was; she told me he was the father of her son. They were separated but lived in the same household. I asked who Ann was, and she said her daughter's name was Andrea. I saw Andrea doing something new with her world—Andrea is working from home and trying to start a new family.

Then Jeanine asked about her friend who had passed away. I first picked up on her grandfather, then picked up on Connie, the friend she'd asked about, whom she had been friends with since they were three years old. I felt Connie was murdered. Jeanine knew it. I felt there was a man involved with Connie's death. She had survived a gunshot wound and lived for six more months. Jeanine and her friend would go and visit Connie all the time in the rehabilitation home. When Connie was still alive, Jeanine would dream about Connie telling her what happened. In the dream, she and Connie were sitting in a truck in a dark area, and Connie would tell her the beginning of the story but would never tell her all the details. The police reported it as suicide, but Jeanine felt there was no way that would have happened; Connie said she was murdered—it was *not* suicide! It was that man, her husband, who did it. I felt that the husband had another girlfriend and wanted to get Connie out of the way. Even Connie's bird, who sounded just like Connie and would repeat everything she said, died shortly after Connie did. Connie's husband was nervous that the bird would say something.

Then I picked up on a *D* sound and asked if the man was D, but then I got the name Eddie or Edward. I told Jeanine that karma was a bitch. She said Ed was not living a very good life at that moment. I said he would have to pay for what he did and even some sociopaths had a little bit of a conscience. Connie's brother tried to open up the case, but the police said they'd lost all the records. This whole time it had been so frustrating because they all knew Ed had done it! It had been haunting Connie's mom and dad and all her loved ones.

Next, I got the initial *M*. I asked if that made sense. Jeanine said Connie's last name, and the parents' last name, was Marshall. I told Jeanine to tell Connie's mom her daughter was doing okay. Their house had just burned down, and it had been really hard. Connie told me that karma would happen to Ed. I told her how I have always seen karma in real time. I think my life's experiences allow that so I can share it with my clients, students, and listeners. Whatever you may not see in reality, it will happen on the other side. What goes around comes around. Connie knew what would happen. She knew the truth. Sometimes people don't get full closure while on Earth, but they get closure when they get to the other side and greet their loved ones.

Nancy called in about her mystical experience, which had happened fifteen years earlier. She'd had a miscarriage five years prior to that and was still very upset about it. The morning of her experience, Nancy was at a spiritual retreat at a convent in New Jersey. She had gone down to breakfast and had come back to her room to rest. Just then, her deceased mother and grandmother appeared and came toward her! She couldn't believe it! She asked herself, *Is this really happening?* Then they came toward her with a little girl. There must have been a great energy at the retreat that allowed the spirits to appear in the daylight. It was an incredible experience.

I started to read for Nancy and picked up on an S and C. I got the names *Steven* and *Sam*. Her living brother was Steven, and her deceased grandfather was Sam. I felt Sam's energy and knew her brother was named after him. Then I saw Rose. I knew it was her aunt.

Nancy said, "I actually just looked at her picture this morning."

I said, "You probably summoned her without even knowing, because looking at her photo brought her loving energy with us tonight."

Just the thought of people we love can bring them to us. Love is the bridge that connects us to the other side. Nancy loved her aunt a lot and was amazed by this whole experience. The spirits were also telling me about an H, and I got the name *Harry*, who was her great-grandfather. I saw that he came through Ellis Island from Russia or Poland. She said he was from Russia or Prussia. I saw them working with food or fruit. An uncle of hers was in the food business. Louis popped in. He was her great-uncle. Then I saw Lea, who was her great-grandmother and Louis's mother. I told her that when we reincarnated, we did so in tribes, so they were all together on the other side. They were watching over Nancy's family. I saw another N, and it was her great-great-uncle Nathan, whom she was named after. He was married to Lea. I saw that Nancy had all the old black-and-white photos. Those people were all around her. They were very brave people.

Later on my show, I said I really felt like we were missing another good story for a near-death experience. My sister had that feeling as well. We took another caller from a Chicago number, but we couldn't hear her voice. I then got a message from the dropped call. She actually had just been on a Netflix special about near-death experiences, so I planned to make her a special guest on Zoom a couple of weeks later. See? Things happen for a reason!

The next caller was from southern Arizona. Her mystical experiences had been from her thirty-six-year-old son after he passed. It's so heartbreaking when someone loses their child. The family hadn't been with her first son when he passed and were unclear about the cause, but before they had gotten word that he'd passed, her son came to her. She could feel him lying on what looked like a cloud, and it was like a shawl wrapped around her shoulders. It was an incredible light. A couple of days later, they received word that he had passed.

The caller's son had come to her several times. Also, his own little son, whom he'd left behind, used to see him as well. My caller saw her son lit up like Christmas lights. When she would walk down the hall and turn the corner to her grandson's room, she would see those same lights arching over her grandson as he slept. She had an instantaneous feeling that her son was looking at him.

She had another experience with her second son, not long after the passing of her first son. Her second son was staying with her, and she had knocked on his door. When she opened the door, she saw those same lights watching over him.

Also, my caller had lost her dog of fifteen years a few days earlier. She was just so upset. She went to the doggy park and didn't know what to do. She was crying her eyes out. Sometimes when she saw the lights of her son, she would get angry and say, "Why are you showing me this? You should be here! Why are you there?"

She has a different attitude about it now. She knows all of us one day will be on that journey, and she knows her son and her dog will be there to greet her, so she's not as afraid of death. When she makes her crossing, she will be excited to greet them.

She sees this now as an experience like when you tell a kid they are going to go to Disneyland the following week. There's an amazing feeling of excitement. It will be a huge adventure. Of course, she said she was going to live her life to the fullest here.

We all will be on our deathbeds one day. When it's that time, we have something to look forward to, as long, of course, as we have lived with love and compassion and kindness and didn't intentionally hurt anyone else. We will reunite with our loved ones who passed on before us. How exciting is that? It helps us let go of our earthly bodies when it is our time. When the body gives up, it is time to move on.

Next, I asked my caller who Mike was, and she said her brother was Michael. Then I saw a *J* or *G*. I got the name *Jennie*. It was her grandmother, who she said was taking care of my caller's son. Then I saw John, her brother. As she got older, she and her sister appreciated Jennie more because they were orphans and were just thrown on Jennie. Their mother died when the caller was four, and though her mother had many siblings, Jennie was kind enough to take them in. Not an easy task. She didn't really want to be their grandmother. However, my caller and her sister have some fond memories. Jennie was probably the best mother they had.

Then I heard a voice talk about Chris. The caller started laughing and said, "Oh my, you are going to out me!" *Chris* was her real name! She didn't like the name *Christine*, and her deceased son used to call her *Christine*! I then picked up on his middle name. I asked if it was John or Michael. She said, "Yes, exactly!" That was the validation: he gave me his middle names and called her *Christine*. Then her son wanted to know where the Christmas tree was. She said she had done nothing for Christmas. Her son loved Christmas and said she still had some of his ornaments from when he was a child. Maybe that was why she got a flash to cut off one of the evergreen branches to take to the country to the house they were going to that night. Then her son wanted her to know he had her dog and was taking care of it till she got there to be with them. She screamed, "Oh my God!" I told her I saw her getting another dog. She said her grandson, her son's son, was still little and she was planning on taking him to the shelter to pick out another dog together—and it would be their dog! I thanked her for trusting me and calling.

After one of my shows, Connie texted me: "As my dad was passing away from cancer, his blue eyes opened so bright. And he said to me, 'Jesus is darker skinned.'" That's the second validation from our callers as to what Jesus really looked like.

The Teacher

I was always interested in astrology. I didn't know much about it, but I liked the idea that it could guide your future. As I have mentioned before, I got married right out of college. I met my ex-husband at a ski lodge in Michigan. In fact, I took skiing as one of my course credits. We lived in the suburbs of Detroit and had a home in northern Michigan, where we produced dinner theater at a restaurant. I was active in community theater as well. He was very supportive of it. I think he liked seeing his wife onstage. I was in *Godspell* and played Nancy in *Oliver!*

On paper, we looked happy, but we were starting to have problems. While in community theater, I met a woman who went to séances. Her name was Judy. Her best friend was a medium. She kept saying, "We are going to talk to a dead Native American man named Red Feather." I was and am always in for an adventure! She invited me to one of the sittings. Now remember, when I was eight years old, I saw a spirit at the foot of my bed and didn't know what it was. Our house had been broken into two weeks before that, and I thought the burglars were living in the attic above my closet. I had to have someone stand in the doorway of my room until I fell asleep with the light on. I went to summer camp for ten years so I wouldn't be alone.

The medium lived in a bad neighborhood in Detroit. I could handle that. I knocked on the back door, and a petite woman with short blond hair answered. I walked in the door and looked to the right in the kitchen. All the walls were red. The stairs were in front of me. She was friendly and walked me downstairs into the basement. I noticed that all the small windows had tinfoil on them. Judy was there, so I felt more comfortable.

The medium said, "Let's go into the séance room." It, too, had tinfoil on the small windows. There was a small card table in the middle of the room. Hanging above it was a red light bulb. There were four of us altogether: Judy, me, the medium, and her mother. Her mother was a lovely lady and was a spiritual healer. I really wasn't sure what I'd gotten myself into. She turned off the light, and it was pitch-black! I grabbed my seat for dear life! I was holding on so tightly that my fingers hurt. Here I was in a bad neighborhood, at a stranger's home in a blackened-out room, and going to talk to a dead spirit guide.

We sat for a while, and the medium said, "Everyone put your fingertips on the table. The table will vibrate and start to move." It was a card table. We sat there for some time. Nothing happened. She said a prayer of protection. Still nothing happened. Then she said, "The spirits like music." So we started singing "Bringing in the Sheaves." I knew the song from going to church every Sunday at camp. I was a good Jewish girl, but I always felt it was important to be open to everyone's beliefs. We sang the song louder, over and over again. Then the table started to vibrate! I wasn't certain if someone was moving it or not. The force of movement on the table got stronger. It actually leaned on one leg. We could feel three legs up in the air even though we couldn't see a thing.

The medium said, "Ask it a question. It will go down on all four legs once for yes and twice for no." So we asked it different questions, and it answered. Needless to say, I was freaked out. But just then, a man's voice started speaking. There were only females in the room! It was a deep man's voice, and he introduced himself as Red Feather. He knew things about me that he couldn't have known. He knew I was unhappy in my marriage even though I had not told anyone. He told me, "One day, you are going to be a famous psychic." I was blown away.

When the evening was over, I felt like I had found a home. I was obsessed with finding out everything I could about psychic work. The next time I went back, the medium and her guide told me I could read. There was a stranger there. I went upstairs with this woman. I had never met her before in my life. I started telling her things about her life that I could not have known about. I knew she was in an unhappy marriage. I saw her work and what she did. I knew names of people close to her, both living and deceased. She was so impressed with what I told her, she told everyone how accurate I was. It was at that moment I had an epiphany! I knew this was going to be my life's work! I always knew I had a purpose on this Earth that would help people. I dedicated my life to it, and fifty years later,

I'm as ambitious to share my knowledge as ever, and I learn something new about it every day!

Meanwhile, my soon-to-be ex-husband was not pleased with my newfound purpose. He also didn't like the medium who became my teacher. She worked during the day as the fundraising director for Easterseals. I was constantly calling her with questions about psychic phenomena and the other side. I would have her on the phone for hours. We only had landlines then. She volunteered me to be the publicist for Easterseals, where I started the ski program for amputees. Those kids were awe-inspiring! I learned so much from them and their positive attitudes!

I put celebrities on TV and radio and in print to promote our fundraisers, and I drove the celebrities around. I told you about the billiard bash with Minnesota Fats and how he kept flirting with me. I was on WWJ radio when I was promoting a fundraising event and the announcer asked what I did. I told him I was a schoolteacher, but I was learning to be a psychic. I went on the radio and talked about my newfound profession. My family and friends were so supportive, except for my husband. When I was on the radio, he listened to it and said, "You'd better go back to speech school!" (My degree from college was teaching speech and English.) Needless to say, our marriage fell apart.

My teacher helped me find a well-known lawyer. He was usually too busy for me, but the day my ex stole my horse was the last straw. I had been pulling my horse out of the trailer that they were trying to put him in, and my ex had thrown me against the barn. I had started crying uncontrollably.

My teacher marched me into the fancy lawyer's office with my shedding white Labrador retriever. His carpet was cobalt blue, but it quickly became blue and white from all the hair my dog was shedding. The lawyer wasn't too busy to come into the waiting room then. That had gotten his attention, and Tevy was licking him and wagging her tail. I then took my dog and cat and boarded them with my veterinarian, who also happened to be my seventh-grade science teacher. I wasn't going to let my ex take them too. A couple of weeks later, the horse was back in my front yard.

By then, I was doing private readings. Word of mouth was my best advertisement. I was—and am—blessed that I have loyal clients. In fact, some of my clients started out with me fifty years ago. As I said earlier in the book, I'm now reading for the third generation, and in some cases, I'm connecting with their grandparents in heaven who originally came to me. I was able to support myself and my animals. I still have my land and the barn in Michigan, though no animals; now I just feed the deer. My parents and family were and are extremely supportive of my work. In fact, in the '70s, my father would take some of my business cards and pass them out to his customers. He had a family business, running a furniture store with my mom and his siblings.

I have described my teacher a few times in this book. As I mentioned, over time as our relationship became less positive, we spoke less frequently. At one point, I found out that she had been in a car accident. I called her as soon as I heard the news, and I spoke to her. Her voice was animated. "Char, I was dead! I was really, really dead! The doctors said my heart stopped. I saw demons! I was in excruciating pain. It smelled like sewers and garbage. Then I was alive again!" She was given a second chance to live with love in her heart. But even though she'd had an NDE, she continued to connect with the dark side.

I know people who went to her classes after that. I had dinner with one of her former students, and he told me he had to stop going to the classes because they became so negative and dark. He said she had later passed away. She was a chain-smoker and did not take care of herself. I forgave her a long time ago. I knew she was not balanced, to say the least. I hope she has found her way up the ladder in the spirit world. She was truly a teacher. She taught me about good and evil by her actions and Jekyll-and-Hyde personality. As I say so often, the world is like a battery: there is always a positive and negative charge.

I have learned that you have to be very protected in a séance. Going into a trance can be extremely dangerous. You never know what energies are entering you. I know that someone whose intention is good and light can turn to evil and dark. My advice is to be careful if someone goes into a trance. If you are involved in a group reading or séance, make sure the person conducting it has a pure energy and is extremely qualified to connect with spirits. Be especially cautious of transmediums, people who allow spirits to speak through them.

Psychic Main Points

* Always be aware of unseen energies around you.
* The Universe will always tip us off when we need to know something.
* Going into a trance can be dangerous if you are not protected!
* Spirit communication is not a toy and needs to be respected.

Psychic Journal Practice

Get your I AM PSYCHIC Journal.

Answer these questions:

* What do others' NDEs teach you about life?
* How can the idea of life beyond life change *your* life?
* How can you use your intuitive abilities to tap into the eternal energy of life?

10

PROTECTION
AND TUNING IN

What you will learn in this chapter: You can harness your psychic intuition to be more empowered. Before tuning in to your psychic intuition, it is most important to say a prayer of protection, to wrap yourself in a blinding white light. Swirl the lights around you like a tornado. Then put yourself inside a mirrored egg. The mirror will deflect anything negative around you.

It's time to prepare yourself for some very practical and very important skills that every intuitive person needs to learn. We'll discuss ways to stay safe as you journey through the energies of the Universe, not all of which wish you well. I cannot stress enough how important it is for you to stay firmly rooted in the protection of love and light!

Let's begin here with the prayer of protection, which I mentioned in Chapter 1.

To recall, the prayer I use is:

*We ask the universal consciousness and God that holds
the highest spiritual power of knowledge, wisdom, and truth to
guide and protect us as we communicate with our guides and
angels in the spirit world and tap into the wisdom of the Universe. We respect this opportunity and take full responsibility to
use this not for ego or controlling others but with the pure intention of spreading love and healing life on this Earth and beyond.*

    *Anything that is in, near, around, or about me that is not
of light, go back to where you came from and turn to light if
you choose—**but stay away from me!***

Make sure you own your power. It is not enough to just
believe you are psychic. In belief, there is doubt. Knowing
means certainty! You must know with all your heart that you
are psychic and intuitive. When you *know* you are psychic and
intuitive, the confidence within will open up your psychic ability to communicate.

It is important to own the four Cs: **courage, confidence,
commitment, conquer.**

Have the courage to pursue this sixth sense that you have and
the confidence to own it! Commit yourself to being aware and to
understanding your ability. Conquer it by acting upon it. You may
be in the busiest part of your day and you get an overwhelming
feeling to call your child, your friend, your mother, your father,
or your spouse, but you are very busy. You may be in a business
meeting and not have time to do this. No matter what, make
the time to follow through on your feeling. Sometimes it can be
a matter of life or death. Perhaps your parent isn't feeling well
and needs your help, or your child needs you to pick them up
from school. Whatever it is, when it's that all-knowing feeling, pay
attention to it and conquer it by acting upon it!

When we are emotionally, spiritually, and physically balanced, the ability to receive and send messages is clearer. Be sure to be balanced in your life. You want to make sure your guidance is coming from the right place. We live in a physical world, and we live in an energetic world. There are good and evil energies in both. When we are balanced, we are more aware of where our messages are coming from. We are all protected, but as I've said earlier, it's like Swiss cheese around us. There are little holes that trickster energies will exploit to try to fool us. So stay in the light and mirrored egg!

Be aware of your thoughts. Thoughts are energy. Thoughts are like radio waves that we use to receive and transmit messages. Thoughts have power. Thoughts have wings. Thoughts create reality. When you are given a message, it is usually not your own thought. It's a thought guided through you from a higher power. It comes through you, not from you. Thoughts are usually the most used method of communicating with spirits.

Negative thoughts attract negative thoughts, and positive thoughts attract positive thoughts. Make it a habit to try to not overthink things. Try to turn negative thoughts to positive thoughts. You don't want trickster energies playing with your mind.

Fear can be a friend or a foe. If you live in fear, you will never know when you are receiving a healing message. It is most important to live with faith. When you live with an attitude of guidance and faith, you will be powerful. If you are living with this power, the Universe will tip you off if you need to know something to prevent a problem or obtain a goal.

In life, there are no coincidences. Things happen for reasons. My best lessons are the ones I learned by my mistakes. When life flows and things work out, it's because they are meant to. There are reasons we have certain experiences in life, good and bad. Life is our school, and we are here to learn lessons.

Your first psychic experience has already happened. Maybe you met someone and your first feeling was not to trust them. Maybe it's a romance, maybe a business opportunity or a friendship. You ignore that first feeling and you get involved with them. You find you have things in common or there's a physical attraction. Time proves your first feeling right, and you suffer the consequences. Or perhaps you did listen and found out later that staying away was a very wise choice and you were being protected!

We use our other five senses along with our feelings to enhance our sixth sense. When something feels right intuitively, you may get goose bumps. You may hear voices before you fall asleep at night. You may smell the perfume or pipe smoke from a loved one who has crossed over.

When tuning in, go straight to the universal consciousness of goodness, love, and God. Make sure you are not allowing trickster energies to get in the way. We all have guardian angels and spirit guides that walk with us. They are here to guide and protect us. Make sure your connection is from a wise, positive place. Remember, spirits are like friends: they can give you good advice and bad advice. So measure your messages received with the highest energy of wisdom, goodness, and love.

There are two ways of being intuitive and psychic: *psychic at random* and *psychic on demand*. *Psychic at random* involves the subtle messages that come in daily life. You have a gut feeling about something that interrupts your daily life in some way. It is important to conquer it by acting upon it.

Psychic on demand is when you want to read someone's energy. It is important to ask permission if you are going to read someone. Allow your mind to go blank. You do not want to get in the way of the messages coming in. Feel the energy of that person and let your nerve endings meet theirs. A thought will come into your mind. It is a thought downloaded into you. It is not a thought you think. The more you do it, the more that feeling will become familiar to you. Your intuition and psychic ability is like a muscle. The more you use it, the stronger it gets. In the beginning, it can be a bit tiring and draining.

Also, if you are being energetically drained, be careful. There are people who are psychic vampires. They will drain you emotionally and psychically. There was once a girl who kept calling me with her problems. I finally told her to go to a therapist. It is up to us to keep boundaries with people. You want to be appreciated!

The most important thing to remember is that the energy of love never dies. When we die, or cross over, we judge ourselves in God's eyes. It doesn't matter how rich, famous, or beautiful we seem. We judge ourselves by our deeds. Even our thoughts. Karma is real. If you think negatively about someone else, it can ricochet back at you. What goes around comes around. Living your life with kindness, empathy, love, and compassion will always get you a first-class ticket to heaven. Like I have said many times before, life is our school, and we are all here to learn lessons. The spirit world is a school as well. It is a place where we can elevate our souls. If you need to ask forgiveness, then do so. It is also important for us to forgive. You never want to carry that toxic energy within you. When you have faith, you will know that the Universe is just. I have truly lived to see karma in real time. I promise you, either here or on the other side, karma happens!

Kathy Hilton's Story

I was asked to be on the popular magazine show *Entertainment Tonight.* They wanted me to read for Kathy Hilton. I was invited to go to her home. Kathy had just given me a book party for *The Universe Is Calling You.* She told the story about how she was skeptical about me reading for her. Kathy always believed in her own intuition but didn't know what to make of me. She asked me to read for her sister Kim. I had no idea I was going to read for her as well. She talked about how I knew so many things about Kim and how impressed she was. I then told Kathy that she would be invited to Buckingham Palace. She thought I was crazy! Two weeks later, she got the invitation to Buckingham Palace. Kathy and her family have become dear friends of mine.

Elizabeth's Story

Elizabeth called my show. She is a hospice nurse. She said that karma can be a positive thing. Another caller had said positive, beautiful things can happen with karma. I said, "That's a good point." Many people are waiting for karma to happen as revenge, but the truth is, what goes around comes around, so the most beautiful experiences in life happen as a result of karma. Elizabeth is on the front lines. She travels a lot. She was so humble about being a hero. She said one of the most difficult things about COVID was when her patients were dying and their families couldn't be with them, so Elizabeth FaceTimed with the families to help them say goodbye to their loved ones.

Elizabeth has coded a lot of people, and they have told her about their near-death experiences. One very powerful experience involved a blind lady. By the time the lady arrived in the unit, she was intubated and sedated. She wasn't really aware of what was going on. Elizabeth was not her nurse, but there were four of them in the room, working to revive her. Elizabeth was doing chest compressions. After the lady came to, she recognized Elizabeth! Even though she had been blind since birth, she knew the badge said Elizabeth's name. She also said she was floating above the room and she could see Elizabeth pushing on her chest. She said there was an instrument up there, like clamps. You could not see them when you were in the room; you could only see them if you were up above the light. Elizabeth said a lot of people will come back to her and say they saw music and felt colors. The blind lady said she saw things, but it wasn't like the vision that others experience. She described it like she could touch things. Not visually, but she could experience them. She described the room as twelve paces across; the bed was in the center, and it was eight paces to the door. There was no way she could have known that! But when she described it from her point of reference, the description was accurate.

I leave you with this: Goodness has more power than evil. But goodness has to work ten times harder to win. To cover a coat of black paint, it takes ten coats of white. To cover a coat of white paint, it only takes one coat of black.

Much of life is about the choices we make. This is a parable I explored in *The Universe Is Calling You*. It deserves repeating.

The Story of Two Wolves

A grandfather is teaching his grandson about life. "A fight is going on inside me," he said to the boy. "It is a terrible fight, and it is between two wolves. One is evil—he is anger, envy, sorrow, regret, greed, arrogance, self-pity, guilt, resentment, inferiority, lies, false pride, superiority, and ego."

He continued, "The other is good—he is joy, peace, love, hope, serenity, humility, kindness, benevolence, empathy, generosity, truth, compassion, and faith. The same fight is going on inside you—and every other person, too."

The grandson thought about it for a minute and then asked his grandfather, "Which wolf will win?"

The old man simply replied, "The one you feed."

Good Charma

I love my spiritual work! I love my life! I have been blessed to have "Good Charma"! I always say if you are not having fun, find another way. I am one of those people fortunate enough to say, "I've never been to work a day in my life." I have learned many lessons in my life. I also learn so much from my clients, my students, and my viewers who call into *CharVision*. Life is what happens to you while you are planning for it. It's important to set goals and work hard to achieve them. If for some reason you are put on a different path, there is always a more divine reason for your purpose in life. Yes, as I have said many times, we are always being tested. We are being given a chance to elevate our souls so that we can become one with the universal consciousness of goodness, love, and God. One of our greatest gifts is to have faith. Faith allows us to have hope to attain our goals in life. Hopefully, we all learn from our mistakes. Some of our most difficult life lessons turn out to be blessings in disguise. We all have the sixth sense of intuition. Some people call it the God voice in their heads. The more we listen, the more we are guided. Remember the four Cs I talk about. Have the confidence and courage as you commit yourself to listening and the guts to conquer and act upon it. And remember, intuition will take you places logic never could.

Psychic Main Points

* Stay true to yourself, and make sure you take time daily to protect yourself from any negative energies.
* Use the four Cs to empower yourself: courage, confidence, commitment, conquer.
* Reread the story of the two wolves. Which wolf do you usually feed? Which wolf will you choose to feed today?

Psychic Journal Practice

Get your I AM PSYCHIC Journal.
Do the following exercises:

* Write some examples of dreams you have had that are guiding you.
* What result did you have after being guided by your dream?
* How did you interpret your psychic message?
* How many times were you inconvenienced by an intuitive message but were grateful that you acted upon it and followed through?
* What questions should the messages answer?

* List people in your life who were important to you and then changed but helped you learn a great life lesson.
* A soul mate is someone who helps your soul to grow. Name people who have helped your soul to grow and what you learned from them.
* List choices that changed your life forever.
* Have you ever had words coming out of your mouth you didn't mean to say? Have you let your emotions stop you from embracing a thought, then learned later you were being guided by a higher power? List those times and circumstances.

Reminder: Life is our school, and we are here to learn lessons. The goal is to elevate your soul to become one with goodness, love, and God.

11

TESTIMONIALS

Here are some testimonials I wanted to share that people have sent me.

From Ellen Black

I have been reading for Ellen Black's family for over forty years. I think they found me from *A.M. LA*. I read for Ellen's mother when she was alive and now Ellen and her daughters. Three generations! It is an honor when people trust me with their families. There's a special bond I have with them. They make me feel like a part of their family. Whenever I read for other families, they make me feel the same way. It is an honor and privilege. These are some of the stories Ellen has shared with me about our time together.

Thirty-six years ago, I owned an upscale gift shop with celebrity couple Aaron and Candy Spelling. Since we were high profile, I almost never would meet with anyone to show me products. I received a phone call and, after hanging up, turned to my brother and said, "I have no idea why I just made an appointment with a woman to show me jewelry." The appointment day came, and I met with two women. As I sat there looking at the jewelry, I began to get chills and strange feelings, and I turned and asked her friend, "Do I know you?"

It was Char, who replied, "No, pretty sure we don't know each other."

We continued, and I kept getting strange feelings. For some unknown reason at the time, I purchased many pieces of Char's friend Diana Basehart's jewelry.

As they were leaving, Char turned around, looked in my eyes, and said, "I need to talk to you."

Char's friend quickly said, "Char, I don't think you can," as Char was in town to film a special and was under contract not to do any readings, but Char said, "I need to speak with her."

Char began to tell me that my mom—whom she was able to name—was not seriously ill and not to be scared, that she was just excited about a big event coming up (I was getting married soon). My mother had a history of strokes and was in bed at the time, and we were worried she was not going to make it. Char continued bringing up her deceased parents, and every passed relative came through. I began to get extremely dizzy, and Char explained to me why and to just relax. Char then began by asking me who the little boy was in my life. I insisted there was no little boy. Char got very quiet and then said, "Oh, it's an accident. He hurt his head." Then after a quiet moment, she said, "Oh no . . . it was brain cancer." She then said, "He wants to tell Charlie his hair is back and he is looking great, dude." I immediately knew what Char was talking about. I was getting married in the next month, and my fiancé's closest cousin had just lost her son to brain cancer.

Char continued asking questions, and I told her, "I have never met the family. I do not know them." Char told me to write down the messages, so I did. Char said Ron, the little boy, wanted to let everyone know he was excited about becoming an uncle. Ron's sister had just had a baby. He wanted Charlie (his father) to know, "I made the flight." I continued to tell Char I had no idea what that meant. She told me to use the word *prisoner* if I were to tell the story.

Char then turned and left. I ran upstairs to call my mother, who was in bed at the time, and we both cried. I then turned to my bookkeeper at the time and said, "I wish I could hug her." Two minutes later, Char reappeared and said she had reached the corner and needed to come back. She walked in and said, "You can hug me," and whispered, "I believe the swan jewelry you purchased is a healing piece." I put all the jewelry on sale. Most every piece sold except the swan, which stayed in the case for a few years.

After our meeting, I was completely confused as to what to do about the messages from this child Ron, as I had never met the mom and was completely worried about calling someone I did not know with messages from her deceased son. Ellen, our cousin, was not functioning well since her son's death. I decided to call, and it was one of the most difficult phone calls I have ever made. I explained what had happened and asked if she would like to know. She immediately started crying and told me she had tried to reach a psychic and was open to hearing. As I told her the story, she let out screams. I told her about making the flight, and she could barely speak. Ron's dream was to fly on a plane and had never done so. Ellen took him right before he passed, but they would not let him fly due to the brain cancer, so telling her he said he made the flight was an amazing message. She also had been referring to herself as "a prisoner" and said that Ron of course had lost his hair and would definitely have said, "I'm looking great, dude."

Fast-forward around five years. My mother had a horrible heart attack and died on the table at Cedars-Sinai. They brought her back, but she was in a coma. One week into my mother's illness, my brother called me and asked me to quickly come to the shop. He opened the back door, and in his hand, he was holding the swan. I grabbed the swan and went running to the hospital. The next several months, I held the swan on every part of my mother's body that was not functioning, and miraculously, it would heal. At one point, my mother's hand was not functioning, and the doctors told me that it would never come back. We called the swan treatment "Swanee treatment" and told the doctor I would do an all-day Swanee treatment. I held the swan on my mother's hand for over eight hours. In front of the doctor, I looked in my mother's eyes and said, "Now open your hand." My mother opened and closed her hand, and I have never seen a doctor almost pass out. The swan would become a bit famous in town, and for many years, people would call to borrow it when a loved one was sick.

Painting Story

My closest cousin died and left me several paintings. I hung one particular painting of a Native American man in my bedroom. Many years later, I was in a group session, and Char said, "You have a guide. Is there a painting of a Native American man?" I told her yes and that I knew exactly what she meant. Later in the session, Char brought up the painting again and said, "You need to look at the painting. There is something there. I think the signature."

I completely forgot, and one day a couple of years later, I was talking to a friend about how much I loved Char and was such a fan. I quickly remembered and ran to the painting, as I had forgotten to look at the signature. The signature on the painting was *Charette*.

Park Story

Over the years, I started to get feelings with certain people I would be speaking with that I needed to bring them to Char. One person named Amy, whom I knew through business but not very well, begged me to bring her. Within a few moments, Char mentioned a man's name and made a gesture like reaching in his belt for a drink. Amy knew immediately that was her late father. Char asked her about a park and made another gesture in a circle, and Amy said, "Yes. He would push me on that carousel every day."

Char asked Amy, "What happened in the park?"

Amy responded, "A lot. We went every day."

Char would not let up and kept saying, "He wants you to tell me what happened."

Amy insisted that she didn't know what Char meant. Char went on to other people but kept coming back. One of the times she came back to it, she said, "He wants you to tell me what happened with the police."

Amy gasped and started crying, saying, "Oh my God. I completely forgot and blocked it out. We found a dead body in the park and had to call the police and bring them to the body." Amy was completely confused and wondered why this would come up, and Char explained, "He wants you to know it's him!"

Alley Story

Over twenty-five years ago, Char asked me, "Do you live or work on an alley?" I said yes, and Char told me to be careful because she saw something happening in an alley but she'd told me this because she believed you could change your fate by being aware. Over the next few years, I moved my office several times . . . each time, there would be an alley, but I never felt that it was *the* alley. My current office is in Beverly Hills, also off an alley, and I had forgotten about the alley story until one night I was there with my daughter Michelle. We were at the office late, and after getting a bit nervous, I said, "Let's get out of here." As we were headed out the back door, I turned and said to my daughter, "Oh my God, this is the alley." I said, "Let's go out the front door." We went out the door, and as I headed to my car and she headed to hers, I heard my daughter yell, "Get in the car!" I looked at her across the alley and got in my car fast. Through my rearview mirror, I saw a man hidden in the corner waiting near the back gate we would have emerged from! He ran, jumped in a car, and drove off.

Another Story from Ellen Black

Over a period of several weeks, my daughter Michelle became extremely depressed. It did not seem like typical depression, and the only thing she would explain was that it felt like death. She kept mentioning my mother, who'd passed, and after a couple of weeks, I went to the safe, took out one of my mother's necklaces, and brought it to my daughter. Michelle called me and asked if I thought it was okay if she changed the chain. I said of course. Michelle continued to cry over the next week, and I suggested that we call Char and maybe that would help. Within moments, Char asked who Marcia was. This was Michelle's grandmother, who told her, "She wants you to know she saw what you did with her jewelry and it's okay. It made her happy." They talked for an hour, and from that day, whatever Michelle had been feeling was lifted.

FBI Story

I had a strong feeling that I should bring one of my friends who was going through a breakup to Char. A day before the meeting, he backed out. I said to him, "Don't worry. Whoever ends up with Char is meant to be there." The next day at work, my friend Jane told me that her closest friend was going through something awful. I quickly said, "Would you like to bring her to Char?" since Jane was already going. We brought her friend, not really knowing what was going on. Immediately, Char mentioned a name none of us knew, except for Jane's friend, who said, "Yes, that is for me." Char looked upset and said, "This is a bad person. He has done bad things, and if you are wondering about him being bad, you are correct." I had no idea, but the FBI had just contacted her because her ex-husband was a bomb suspect with ties to a terrorist organization and she did not know what to believe.

Aunt Story

During one of my visits, Char asked me, "Whose hair is falling out around . . . Harlan?" It was first off amazing because my uncle's name was so unusual, and I could not believe Char said that name. This was my aunt Felice, who had just found out days before that she had breast cancer. Char told me to write this down and also said that she did not give out medical advice but to check with my doctor. She said, "If this were me, I would take essiac, and it would be her protectant!"

I called immediately, and after years went by, I completely forgot about it. Five years later, I asked my aunt if she ever got the essiac. She said that she had and in fact was still taking it to that very day and had given it to her housekeeper for her husband, who was given only six months to live—and he was still alive to that day. This was twenty years ago, and my aunt is still going strong!

From Robin Dearden

I have been reading for Robin for over thirty years. She is someone whom I consider to be a lifelong friend. She is naturally intuitive and open, which always makes it easier for me to read. I appreciate that she has trusted me for all these years.

On February 3, 2014, my dear friend Louan passed away. She was one of the most loving, giving, creative people I've ever met. And her death left me with so many questions. I've known Char for over thirty-five years. Whenever I had an unsolvable question, she would be the one I'd call. When I was in my twenties, it would be, "Will I get back together with my boyfriend?" As I got older, my questions got deeper and more important to me.

So when Louan passed, it was time to get some answers. When I called Char, she immediately told me Lou's name and knew that she had died of cancer. Then she said, "She's in a really great neighborhood!" which made me smile. She was good! Char told me that her dad, Rodger, was with her—he had passed a few years before—and then she described Lou to perfection! I knew she would come to Char right away, because she was a very spiritual, intuitive person.

Char told me about Louan's family and friends and husband. As I furiously wrote down her reading, I realized that I could share this good news with everyone in her life. As we were wrapping up, Char said, "Louan's holding a small dog in her arms." She didn't have a small dog. "His name starts with a *B*." I thought, *Well, you can't get them all right.* As I got in my car, I called Lou's husband and told him everything Char said. We were both crying. It was bittersweet but joyful, too, knowing that Lou was "in a good neighborhood." Before I hung up, I said, "Char said Lou was holding a small dog with the letter *B* in its name. But I told her Lou never had a small dog." Her husband gasped and said, "Bernie was our dog at the beginning of our relationship. She loved him more than anything!" I didn't know, but Char did!

From Dorothy Lucey

I met Dorothy doing a reading for her, and as she'll tell you, our first encounter was memorable! I always appreciated how open she was and how trusting. I love her like a sister. Dorothy also introduced me to UBNGo and Tony Sweet. She had a strong feeling about it, which gave birth to *CharVision*.

Char told me I was getting fired. It was my first day on the job. I was hosting a TV talk show. She was my first guest. She shook my hand and said, "You won't be here long." And soon after, my ass was out the door. She also told me, "Something good is coming." The something good was *Good Day LA*, a morning show I hosted for almost twenty years. Char often predicted good things for me, like my son. Before him, I had two miscarriages, one while doing two TV shows. I'd host *Good Day LA* in the morning and then a syndicated show in the afternoon. I hadn't told anyone at work I was pregnant, so I didn't tell them about the miscarriage. I just cried in the bathroom and faked a smile. We had a psychic on. As the segment was ending, she turned to me and said, "It was a girl." I thought I'd cry, vomit, faint—or all three—on TV. Soon after that, I saw Char. She immediately saw dead people. She said, "Who are Sadie and Sonny?" They were my husband's aunts; both had passed. She said, "They want you to see your doctor, have a certain test." I'd already seen my doctor, already had a bunch of tests. I didn't go. Char called me. The dead aunts were bugging her. She said, "Go back to your doctor." I went. I had another test. They figured out why I was having miscarriages. And not much later, I had Nash. I always say he's Char's baby. She'd come over for playdates. She and Nash would take pots and pans out and parade around the house and sing "Parade of the Wooden Soldiers."

Char sang this again for him when he graduated college. I always joke that she got me fired. But she also got me my son.

From My Sister Alicia

You have heard me speak about Alicia many times through-out this book. I am so lucky to have her and my other sister, Elaine, in my life. They are both healers, too, and we have a deep connection to each other that I know many siblings have. You have heard me say many times throughout this book how much I believe in listening to children, and I'm always so grateful to my parents for trusting my intuition even when I was at a young age, as that further instilled a level of trust and connection between my sisters and me, and they have been my biggest supporters.

About fifteen years ago, I received a call from California to Michigan, where I live, at about 9:30 p.m. My sister told me to immediately call our doctor and that my husband Paul's life was in danger. She was worried he was going to have a heart attack. She said there was something wrong with the medication he was taking. I reassured her that he had just changed doctors, was on a new medication, and was fine. She insisted that I call the doctor, and I had learned that I must listen to her, because she is always right. I called the doctor, and he met Paul at the office at 7:30 the following morning. He went through all Paul's medication, and lo and behold, the pharmacist had made a mistake and had given him triple the amount of one that he was supposed to take. Indeed, this high dose of thyroid medication in combination with his heart medicine would have caused a heart attack. She saved his life. We always listen to my sister Char. When she feels something strongly, she is always right. We are so lucky to have her for a sister. She is truly a gift from God.

Class at Lauren King's

One of my dearest friends is Lauren King.

Lauren recalls the night I went to her house to teach some of her friends about intuition. Everyone got there late, and we had dinner. Afterward, some people had to leave. We went into the great room. And everyone sat down and asked me to do a few readings. There were only twelve people there.

Char got the names right for every person. She got M and said *Milton*, who was my dad, was with Mary, who was his mom. Char told me my husband was having pulmonary issues. We started testing immediately, and it still took some months to figure it out. He almost died and probably would have if it weren't for Char's medical intuition.

The next person Char read was Cynthia. She said, "Bud" (that was Cynthia's husband), and then she said that he had a heart problem. Cynthia said she knew, but the best doctor was in San Francisco, and they were going to Sun Valley for a holiday and then San Francisco after the trip. Char told her not to wait, so they went directly to the doctor. Her husband had a 98 percent blockage! He had the operation right away. Char probably saved his life! More magical things happened that night, and it was an amazing experience.

Do you have a sign that your loved ones can identify with when you pass away? My longtime client Michelle was very close to her mother. Her mother had cancer for many years, and it was a miracle she lived so long. Michelle's aunt and mother came up with a sign that she would present once she was in heaven. They decided that Char would figure it out. (Not too much pressure.) Michelle and her aunt called me. I spelled out *head* and then saw Head Board! Thank God for the Universe and my spirit guides for helping me out! I know it brought a sense of peace to them. They knew their beloved was with them!

EPILOGUE

Dear Reader,

Thank you for taking this journey into your intuition with me. I've tried to give lessons, ideas, principles, and more, to help you connect with your own intuition and your loved ones, spirit guides, and guardian angels. I've also shared with you many stories from my own life, my experiences with others, and other people's experiences as well. These stories aren't meant to only entertain you—they are specifically to give you knowledge that can help you on your own intuitive journey.

My hope for you is that you take this instruction, use your I AM PSYCHIC Journal, ask yourself the many questions throughout the book, and explore your own intuition. Don't just take my word for things—try them for yourself, live them, and pay close attention to what happens.

And I've stressed many times to keep yourself protected in the light and love of life. Not all energy is positive, and some negative energy appears positive on the surface. Protecting yourself is the way not to experience negative energy. Come from a mind state of love, not fear, not anger, and not from your ego.

You are a beloved creation of life itself. You deserve all of the love that life wants to show you. Open yourself up to this love, and experience it more and more each day. Life is eternal, and you can put yourself on the path of love with every choice you make, starting today, starting now.

Know that I send you my own love and that I believe in you. Now it's your turn. We each are responsible for our own lives, and I hope that inspires you to live a life that your intuition is no doubt already guiding you toward . . . toward your purpose, toward more love, toward connecting with all of the energy of the Universe.

Love & Light,
Char

APPENDIX

As we conclude these chapters, I want to leave you with some final Q and As to help you along your intuitive journey:

How do I find my spirit animal?

Some people just know automatically who their spirit animal is. If you keep seeing or hearing about an animal and it rings true to you, it usually is.

Do pendulums work?

Spirits do take over pendulums. The problem with them is that pendulums can fool you. It's like a Ouija board sometimes. It can give you inaccurate information. If you are positive that the spirit guide you trust is on it, sometimes they can work, but you cannot rely on them.

You must ask the highest spiritual knowledge of wisdom and truth to guide you. If the person using it is pure and powerful it can bring guidance. Always check the answer with your divine truth and guidance. The more powerful and protected the user, the more accurate the answer.

How do I use a crystal ball?

Always say the prayer of protection before any kind of reading. The first focal point I ever used was a crystal ball. I couldn't afford one, so I made one out of mineral oil and a fish bowl. Did you ever read clouds as a child? It is the same with the crystal ball. Images will appear, and you have to interpret what they mean. Sometimes initials will appear as well. The interpretation is the hardest part for some.

Whatever image comes up in the crystal ball, ask questions. Why is that image there? What does it mean? Who does it pertain to? Or you can ask a question that you want an answer for. Ask the question, and then see what image comes up in the ball. Be confident, and you will figure out the answer.

How do I know if I am psychic?

Everyone is psychic and intuitive. You just have to own the power and trust your feelings and thoughts.

How do I know if a psychic is real?

When getting a reading, they should tell you something they couldn't know about you that is not general. You always want to make sure the person is pure of heart and doesn't want to control you.

No one and nothing has power over you unless you give it to them. Not a living person or a spirit.

What does it mean to be in between reincarnations?

It means you are in the spirit world waiting to get your orders to come back. Some people waiting in the spirit world have jobs to do, like helping others understand they have passed away from the Earth plane into the spirit realm.

How do I know what my past life is?

Sometimes we have memories of other lifetimes. We also bring gifts with us from other lifetimes. Otherwise, explain a three-year-old being able to play Chopin on the piano. My sister Dr. Alicia Tisdale, Ph.D., does past-life regressions. You can also read books by Dr. Brian Weiss.

What is a twin flame?

A twin flame is an intense soul connection thought to be the person's other half. It's based on the idea that sometimes one soul gets split into two bodies. The relationship can be both challenging and healing.

How do I know if am in a karmic relationship? Is it unfinished business?

Many times, we have unfinished business with certain people, and we need to finish our soul's purpose with them.

Why am I not with the love of my life?

Sometimes we think someone is the love of our life and they really are not. Be careful what you ask for: you may get it. Or maybe someone is the love of your life and you will be together the next time around. There are always lessons to learn from these and all relationships.

Do we choose our parents?

Yes, we choose our parents to learn life's lessons and fulfill our karma with those souls. Some of us luck out, and some of us don't.

Do people go to hell?

Water seeks its own level. I believe that some people go to

a dark place and some to an enlightened place. However, the ones who go to the dark place have to work their way through the suffering to get to the light. That's why it is so important to live with a clear conscience, love, compassion, and kindness.

What is a chakra?

We have seven major energy centers in our bodies that need to be fine-tuned to balance ourselves. Each one of our chakras resonates with a color and musical note. I had music composed to balance your chakras. It is called *Chakra Therapy with Char Margolis.* You can download it on Amazon Music, Apple Music, iTunes, CD Baby, and more. You can also purchase the CD from Char.net.

Can I connect with a dead relative?

Yes, many loved ones will show us signs that they are around. Some come in the form of a butterfly, hummingbird, or dragonfly. Some will come as the scent of their perfume or favorite recipe.

How do I know if my spouse is cheating on me?

Sometimes people are drawn to their spouse's phone and find a text or voice mail. Sometimes you just get a strong feeling about it, but it's easy to go into denial because you don't want it to be true. The Universe always tips us off when we need to be warned about something.

What does 11–11 mean?

It's known that you can make a wish when you see this. It means you are in sync with the universal energy.

How do we know who will meet us in heaven?

Many people on their deathbeds start talking to their loved ones who passed before them. I have a concept that the reason our eyes go in the backs of our heads when we pass is because we are following the white light and the spirits who have come to get us.

How do we talk to our spirit guides?

Just start communicating with them. You may not get an answer right away, but when you least expect it, a message will come through. It may be a powerful thought or a dream or another person who cares about you. The more you connect with your guides and the universal knowledge of goodness, God, and love, the stronger your guidance will be.

ACKNOWLEDGMENTS

Over my fifty years of work as a spiritual psychic intuitive medium, there have been many great souls that have contributed to the journey. A huge thanks to my incredible, gifted editor, Joel Fotinos, his patient assistant, Gwen Hawkes, and also the copy editor, Sara Ensey, and the production editor, Melanie Sanders. My gratitude to my publicist, John Karle. A special thanks to Jennifer Enderlin for her continued support of my work, and a big thanks to the entire St. Martin's Press family. It takes a village. Thanks to my trusted attorney, Chase Mellen III, and my manager, Gina Rugolo Judd. My deepest gratitude to my bookkeeper, Nicole Palazzola, for her tireless energy and to her colleague, Jill Palazzola, for helping me.

Friends and family are the most important part of my life. I am so grateful to Evelyn Krasnow, who helped with edits and is like family to me. A special thanks to my nephew Larry Tisdale and his son Jason, and unending thanks to my sisters, Alicia Tisdale (whose constant encouragement and guidance helped mold the book) and Elaine Lippitt, for keeping the goodness and purity of our parents' love alive. Thanks as well to their families and all my amazing friends: Chris Colfer (whom I adore) for his heartwarming friendship and heartfelt foreword, Kathy Hilton for her loving friendship, and my darling Ross Mathews. Special love to Lauren King, Teran Davis, Dorothy

Lucey, and Danny Fantich. Thanks to Stuart Krasnow for his loving friendship, generosity, and support. To those friends who are not mentioned: you know who you are. You know that I love you and am grateful for our friendship. Yes, you too, Becky!

To Tony Sweet for helping to make *CharVision* a success. Thank you to RuPaul, Tom Campbell, and everyone at World of Wonder. A special thank-you to Kelly Ripa, Ryan Seacrest, Michael Gelman, Ed Connolly, and everyone at *Live with Kelly and Ryan* for their continued support, and to my friend Joanne Saltzman. My thanks to Carla Pennington, Brad Bessey, Ellen Black, and Robin Dearden. There are countless people in the media and press around the world that have helped me get my work out, especially in the U.S., Canada, and the Netherlands. You are not forgotten.

Thank you to my colleagues and friends John Edward, Katrina Poulous, Glynis McCants, and Patti Negri! I appreciate all my amazing healers who keep me going, including Dr. Jeffrey Nusbaum, Dr. David Brownstein, Angela, Julie, and Dr. Jeffery Fantich. I am blessed with amazing neighbors who are always there for me, including Cathy, Jim, Jan, Geoffrey, Fred, and Andrew. I can't forget my psychic sidekick, Sunny Margolis, who shows me unconditional love every day!

As always, my deepest thanks go to the thousands of people who have opened their lives and hearts to me and given me the privilege of reading for them and teaching them. To the viewers and listeners of *CharVision* whose stories are an integral part of this book: I hope they will inspire readers one-tenth as much as they have touched and inspired me. Their examples remind us of the goodness, wisdom, and love that connect us all.

ABOUT THE AUTHOR

Paul Smith

CHAR MARGOLIS is an internationally acclaimed intuitive psychic medium who has been stunning audiences for decades with her gift of connecting with the spirit world. She also teaches psychic intuition and helps her students to enrich their lives. Her popular vid/podcast, *CharVision*, can be viewed around the world. In it, she explores all things metaphysical, spiritual, and paranormal while taking live callers and doing readings. She has been on numerous talk shows, including *Live with Kelly and Ryan*, *Dr. Oz*, *Dr. Phil*, and *The Today Show*. She is the author of several books, including *The Universe Is Calling You*. She divides her time among Michigan, Los Angeles, and Palm Springs, California.

For inquiries about private readings, group readings, psychic intuition classes, or speaking events, contact Char at www.char.net.

Follow Char on:

YouTube: CharMargolisPsychicIntuitiveMedium

Facebook: IntuitiveMediumCharMargolis

Twitter: @PsychicMedmChar

Instagram: @charmargolis

TikTok: @charmargolis